ALSO BY ITAMAR RABINOVICH

Syria Under the Ba'th

The War for Lebanon, 1970–1983

The Brink of Peace

The Road Not Taken: Early Arab-Israeli Negotiations

WAGING PEACE

WAGING PEACE

Israel and the Arabs at the End of the Century

ITAMAR RABINOVICH

Farrar, Straus and Giroux / New York

Farrar, Straus and Giroux
19 Union Square West, New York 10003

Copyright © 1999 by Itamar Rabinovich
Distributed in Canada by Douglas & McIntyre Ltd.
Printed in the United States of America
Designed by Jonathan D. Lippincott
First edition, 1999

Library of Congress Cataloging-in-Publication Data
Rabinovich, Itamar, 1942–
    Waging peace : Israel and the Arabs at the end of the century /
Itamar Rabinovich.
        p.   cm.
    ISBN 0-374-10576-6 (alk. paper)
    1. Arab-Israeli conflict—1993– —Peace.   I. Title.
DS119.76.R33   1999
956.95'3044—dc21   99–17464

In memory of my mother,
Tova Buchsbaum Rabinovich

CONTENTS

FOREWORD

During the years 1992–96 I was privileged to serve as Israel's ambassador in Washington and also as its peace negotiator with Syria. In this dual capacity I was especially active on the Syrian track of the Israeli-Arab peace process and also took part in most of its other aspects. This unique opportunity to acquire a much deeper understanding of both the Arab-Israeli conflict and the peace process was grafted onto more than two decades of academic study of and writing on Israel's relationship with the Arab world. So when I returned to Tel Aviv University in September 1996 I decided to write two books: a specific account of Israel's relationship with Syria (this was published in 1998); and an overview of Israel's relationship with the Arab world, which is the present volume.

It is a pleasant duty to thank the institutions and individuals that helped me in the writing of this book: Tel Aviv University, my academic home; the Dayan Center and my friends and colleagues on its faculty and staff; the Yona and Dina Ettinger Chair; and Mrs. Lydia Gareh, Efrat Harel, and Dorit Moshkovits, who helped with research and typing. I am also very grateful to the whole staff at Farrar, Straus and Giroux, and especially to Elisabeth Sifton for her help with the manuscript.

I want particularly to thank my immediate family— Efrat, Iris, Orna, Uri, Itai, and Uri. This month we mark the thirteenth anniversary of the passing away of my mother, to whose memory this book is dedicated. For us the pain of her absence is as acute today as it was in 1986.

Itamar Rabinovich

Tel Aviv, March 1999

WAGING PEACE

THE BACKGROUND

The Arab-Israeli conflict has crossed the half-century mark. A conflict between the small Jewish and the much larger Arab community in Palestine had first erupted in the late Ottoman period. It became fiercer and more significant after the First World War, the publication in 1917 of the Balfour Declaration, in which the British government supported the "establishment in Palestine of a national home for the Jewish people," and the establishment in 1920 of a British Mandate over Palestine on both sides of the Jordan River. During the next three decades, Arabs and Jews fought over rights and control, their conflict culminating in a war that broke out after the United Nations' decision in 1947 to partition the country between a Jewish state and a Palestinian-Arab one.[1]

Throughout the decades of conflict, the indigenous Palestinian Arabs were supported and helped by a large part of the Arab world, but it was the establishment of the state of Israel in 1948 and the invasion by five Arab armies

that gave birth to the full-fledged Arab-Israeli conflict. Israel's victory, the consolidation of its existence and expansion of its original territory, the Arabs' military defeat, the
failure to establish the Palestinian Arab state envisaged by
the UN resolution, and the consequent problem of Palestinian refugees were the fundamental facts in the process
that transformed the Arab-Jewish conflict in Mandate
Palestine into the Arab-Israeli conflict we still know today.

The conflict's fifty-year history is evenly divided by the
October War of 1973. For twenty-five years, the old
wounds festered as efforts to heal them or at least address
some of their causes failed for reasons that I shall analyze.
But after the Israeli victory in October 1973, diplomatic
procedures were inaugurated that four years later developed into an Israeli-Egyptian peace process, which in
March 1979 produced Israel's first peace treaty with an
Arab state, though this subsequently came to a grinding
halt; the stasis lasted through the 1980s. Then a new phase
of peace negotiations was inaugurated in October 1991 at
the Madrid Conference. The ensuing set of negotiations
gave birth to a second Arab-Israeli peace treaty in 1994,
with Jordan, to a Palestinian-Israeli breakthrough, and to a
significant degree of Arab-Israeli normalization; but even
in its heyday in 1993–95 the "Madrid process" failed to
bring about a comprehensive settlement of the Arab-
Israeli conflict or to end the political disputes and the
bloodshed between Israel and parts of the Arab world.
New developments in 1996 slowed it down and in 1998
brought it near collapse.

The Madrid process represents the first sustained international effort to resolve the Arab-Israeli conflict.[2] It is
significant that no comparable effort—as distinct from

short-lived attempts, various mediation efforts, and partial settlements—had been undertaken before, and that twenty-five years of an uneven peace process have still failed to produce a comprehensive settlement. The Arab-Israeli conflict has indeed been one of the more complex and difficult international problems of the second half of the twentieth century. The first step to understanding its complexity is a recognition that there is no single Arab-Israeli dispute but a cluster of distinct, interrelated conflicts:

(1) The core conflict between Israel and the Palestinians. This is a classic conflict between two national movements claiming title to and vying for possession of the same land. This original strand in the Arab-Israeli dispute was overshadowed for some fifteen years (1949–64) by the pulverization of the Palestinian community that had been dispersed during Israel's war of independence, and by the pre-eminence then of pan-Arab ideologies and Arab state interests. The resurgence of Palestinian nationalism in the mid-1960s and, ironically, the establishment in 1967 of Israeli control over the whole of Palestine west of the Jordan River restored a major role to the Palestinians in the Arab world. Their new importance was reinforced by the PLO's offensive against Israel, conducted with the defeat of the established Arab armies in the background.

(2) A broader dispute between Israel and Arab nationalism. This is a national, political, cultural, and increasingly also religious conflict. Both sides came into this conflict carrying their historical and cultural legacies. The Jewish people's national revival in their historic homeland in the immediate aftermath of the Second World War and the Holocaust, and after millennia of exile and persecution,

unfolded during a head-on collision with an Arab national movement seeking revival, renewal, and power after a century of soul-searching and humiliation at the hands of Western powers. Unfortunately, most Arabs have perceived Zionism and Israel as either part of the West or, worse, a Western bridgehead established in their midst.

(3) A series of bilateral disputes between Israel and neighboring Arab states created by geopolitical rivalries combined with other factors. Thus Egypt was drawn into war with Israel in 1948 by the Palestinian problem, but its decision to join the Arab war coalition and its subsequent conflict with Israel were also affected by the ambitions of Arab and regional leaders, by its sense of competition with Israel as the other powerful and ambitious state in the region, and by a desire to obtain a land bridge to the eastern Arab world through the southern Negev Desert. Similarly, Syria's bitter relationship to Israel has expressed both its genuine attachment to Arab nationalism and to the Palestinian cause, and its acute sense of rivalry with Israel for hegemony in the Levant.

(4) The larger international conflict. The "Palestine question" has always been an important and a salient international issue. The interest and passion aroused by the "Holy Land" (*Falastin* to Arabs and Muslims), the saliency of what used to be called the "Jewish question," the rivalries of colonial powers and later the superpowers in the Middle East, and the overall geopolitical importance of the Arab world were some of the considerations and forces that have accounted for the significance in international affairs of the evolving Arab-Israeli conflict. It was not originally and was never allowed to be a local squabble. Arabs and Israelis from the outset sought interna-

tional support for their respective causes, while foreign governments and other actors—out of genuine commitment to one of the parties, in search of gain, or for the sake of peace and stability—have always intervened.

These international factors were magnified and exacerbated by the Cold War. The Middle East, because of its intrinsic importance, its geographical closeness to the Soviet Union, and its openness to change, became an important arena of Soviet-American competition. In the early 1950s, the Soviet Union shifted from initial support for Israel to sweeping support for the Arab states, and it exploited the Arab-Israeli conflict in order to weaken the Western position in the Middle East and enhance its own. After about a decade of fluctuation, the United States decided on a policy of open cooperation with Israel and other Middle Eastern allies against the region's radical and pro-Soviet regimes. So, in the Arab-Israeli wars in 1967 and 1973 and in other Middle Eastern crises, the two superpowers contended by proxy. Israel's power was increased dramatically by American aid and support, but the Soviet Union's military assistance to its allies and clients, the prospect of Soviet military intervention, and Soviet help in rebuilding the defeated Egyptian and Syrian armies were important in denying Israel the political fruits of its military power and achievements.[3]

Whereas in the 1950s and early 1960s it was the Soviet Union that tended to take advantage of the Arab-Israeli conflict, the equation was altered by Israel's victory in the 1967 war. Within a few years, the Arab world grasped that the key to regaining the territories Israel had gained in that war was to be sought in Washington. American endorsement of the principle of exchanging "land for peace," and a willingness and ability to act on it, were at least some of the time the basis on which the United States was able to orchestrate the Arab-Israeli peace negotiations and register several impressive achievements. For example, the Egyptian-Israeli peace process initiated after the 1973 war, the first major breakthrough in the Arab-Israeli conflict, was intimately linked to one of Washington's greatest Cold War accomplishments: Egypt's transition from a Soviet ally to a nation in the American orbit.[4]

1948–67

This was the formative period of the Arab-Israeli conflict. The 1948 war which gave birth to both the state of Israel and the Arab-Israeli conflict ended with a series of armistice agreements, not with a peace settlement. This fact has in recent years been the focus of a fierce debate in Israel among three schools of opinion: an orthodox, establishment-oriented, sometimes almost official historiography which blames this failure on the Arab world and its refusal to accept Israel's existence; a revisionist school which considers these critical years through a contemporary ideological prism, relying on several newly opened archives, primarily Israel's state archives, and which lays much of the blame on Israel and its leader, David Ben-Gurion, for refusing any sensible compromise or concession; and a further school of post-revisionists, also using newly available archival and other sources, which shuns both the apologetic tendency of the first historiography and the blunt revisionism of the second.[5]

This third group is interested less in allocating blame and discovering "missed opportunities" than in trying to understand the stalemate produced by the Arab-Israeli clash of interests and outlooks and in their asymmetries. Israel sustained heavy casualties in the 1948 war, believed that in the aftermath of the Holocaust the Jewish people was entitled to a secure homeland, and maintained that a belligerent force defeated in a war that it had itself initiated could not reasonably demand a reversal of its outcome.

Israel was also guided by a genuine, albeit sometimes exaggerated, existential insecurity and a fear that a "second round" might be initiated by its Arab adversaries, who had refused to accept the war's outcome and Israel's entrenchment in their midst. Under Ben-Gurion's leadership, Israel sought to stabilize the status quo, on the assumption that, once it had consolidated its existence and absorbed the postwar wave of Jewish refugees and immigrants, peace could be made on better terms a few years later. In a series of exploratory and then real peace negotiations conducted after the 1948 war, Israel offered some concessions, though not the ones demanded by its Arab interlocutors.[6]

From the Arab nationalist perspective, Israel was an illegitimate state that threatened the Arab world culturally and geopolitically. The few Arab leaders who agreed to negotiate with Israel insisted on far-reaching concessions (giving up the southern part of the Negev Desert, allowing a corridor to link Gaza to the West Bank, permitting the return of Palestinian refugees, jurisdiction over part of Lake Tiberias), both in order to legitimize any prospective agreement in Arab eyes, and because they believed that

only significant and painful Israeli concessions could re-
dress some of the injustices done them by Israel's very establishment and the expansion of its original territory, the
defeat of the Arab armies, and the disintegration of the
Palestinian community.[7]

A close look at the various attempts to arrive at peace
settlements between Israel and its Arab neighbors after
the 1948 war will point to many reasons and forces responsible for their failure, but at the root of the difficulty
lay the truth that the Arab and Israeli perspectives were
irreconcilable. In the circumstances obtaining at the war's
end, any concession that could possibly satisfy at least
some of the Arabs was perceived by Israel's leaders as an
existential threat. This state of affairs continued until June
1967, when Israel's victory in the Six-Day War gave it territorial assets that it could use as bargaining chips in peace
negotiations. Until then, the conflict had lingered and festered. The limitations and shortcomings of the armistice
agreements, friction over unresolved issues, the impact of
radical ideologies espoused by certain Arab army officers
on Arab politics, Israel's response to these developments,
and the Soviet Union's influence in the region combined
to shape a full-blown Arab-Israeli conflict by the mid-
1950s. This meant a virtual absence of normal contacts between Israel and the Arab world; a complete Arab boycott;
border clashes; individual and organized group Arab
violence against Israel and an Israeli policy to retaliate
against both; a second Israeli-Arab war in 1956 shaped by
Israel's cooperation with Great Britain and France, two
declining colonial powers, versus revolutionary pan-Arab
nationalists; an arms race; and perennial fear of still more
war.[8]

Soon events and developments occurred that led to the crisis of May 1967 and the Six-Day War in June. One was the completion of Israel's overland water carrier, bringing water from Lake Tiberias in the north to the more spacious but arid lands in the south, and the Arab decision to thwart a project designed to enhance Israel's absorptive capacity and thus consolidate its existence. A second was the return of the Palestinians and the Palestinian national movement to a directly active role in Middle Eastern politics with the emergence of various groups and organizations that subsequently assembled under the umbrella of the Palestine Liberation Organization. Third was the radicalization of Syrian politics under the Ba'ath Party's regime and the exacerbation of rivalries among various Arab states, particularly with regard to issues relating to Israel. Fourth was the intensification of Soviet-American rivalry in the region. And lastly there was a leadership crisis in Israel after David Ben-Gurion's second and final abdication in 1963.[9]

1967–73

Though the June 1967 war created a potential for a political settlement by gaining Israel new territorial assets, it also escalated the Arab-Israeli conflict to hitherto unfamiliar levels. Right after the war, Israel indeed considered the Sinai Peninsula and the Golan Heights as, essentially, temporary holdings to be used in order to obtain a genuine peace, but as time went by and peace failed to come, the situation progressively acquired the trappings of permanency, and the temporary holdings were tied to Israel by a variety of bonds and vested interests.

The West Bank and the Gaza Strip, which Jews considered parts of the historical Land of Israel and which had been parts of Mandate Palestine, were treated from the outset on an entirely different basis. Sovereignty over the West Bank and Gaza was, unlike that over the Sinai and the Golan, according to the Israeli interpretation at least, an open issue. Control over and title to these territories raised fundamental issues of security and identity—these were the lands of the Bible (much more so, in fact, than the coastal plains where most of Israel's population actually lived). In them lay the key to a historic compromise with Palestinian nationalism or, alternatively, to yet another effort to make an agreement with Hashemite Jordan; but neither the shape of such a settlement nor an available partner was readily apparent. Moreover, Israel's politics were altered by the powerful wave of messianic-mystical nationalism generated by Israel's acquisition of Judea and Samaria. (In the coded language of Israeli politics, the term "West Bank" is neutral but the biblical term "Judea and Samaria" expresses a claim to the heartlands of Jewish history.) This wave was reinforced by the Israelis' unprecedented sense of power after their great and swift military victory, and their determination never to return to the vulnerable borders of the prewar period or to a trauma like the one they had endured in May 1967.[10]

The military might that Israel displayed in June 1967 convinced the Arabs that they could not reasonably hope to end the conflict through a military victory. The effect of the 1967 defeat was qualitatively different from that of the defeats in 1948 and 1956—Israel's swift and stunning victory could not be explained away by the Western powers' direct participation or by the decay of the old order in the Arab world, for though King Hussein was a traditional Arab monarch, the Nasserite regime in Egypt and the Ba'ath regime in Syria were paragons of revolutionary Arab nationalism. In the Arabs' ensuing soul-searching, several alternatives were fiercely debated—return to the Islamic fold, further radicalization, staying with the familiar status quo. But a recommendation to draw yet another conclusion from the repeated failure to defeat Israel—to seek a political settlement based on a historic compromise—was not made.[11]

These Israeli and Arab frames of mind were chiefly responsible for the diplomatic stalemate over the next six years. Meanwhile, the Soviet Union hastened to rebuild and resupply the Egyptian and Syrian armies, while the United States supported Israel's insistence that its victory should lead to nothing less than a genuine settlement of the Arab-Israeli conflict. The UN's lengthy deliberations in the summer and fall of 1967 ended with the adoption of Security Council Resolution 242, an epitome of "constructive ambiguity": it has served ever since as the basis for the several efforts to resolve the Arab-Israeli dispute precisely because its careful formulation (along with the differences between the English, French, and Russian versions of it) has enabled all parties to claim the validity of their own interpretations.

The initial efforts at international mediation having failed, Egypt, with its armed forces rehabilitated with Soviet aid, resumed hostilities in late 1968. Limited fighting with Israel spread along the Jordanian and Syrian fronts; this "war of attrition" lasted until the summer of 1970.

The Arab states' eagerness to regain the territories they had lost in June 1967 was supplemented and enhanced by Palestinian nationalism's quest for self-determination. Thus the Six-Day War gave new scale and impetus to a process that had already begun: the Arab states' formation of the original PLO, the challenge presented to the PLO by authentic Palestinian groups, the formulation of the Palestinian National Charter—in short, the return of the Palestinian issue to the forefront of the Arab-Israeli conflict.

After the June war, the relationship and balance between the Palestinian national movement and the Arab states changed, the latter losing power and prestige while the former seemed to offer new hope—of defeating Israel through a popular war of liberation, and inflicting unfamiliar blows on it through a series of spectacular terrorist acts. In addition, the Palestinians built virtually independent territorial bases in Jordan and Lebanon, at the expense of these states' sovereignty. Authentic Palestinian organizations led by Yasser Arafat and the Fath took control of the PLO, ending the duality of the previous four years. Arafat became an important Arab leader, wielding influence in summit conferences and at other Arab meetings.[12]

In theory, some of these developments might have been the basis for an Israeli-Palestinian accommodation. Israel was in control of all of Mandate Palestine, but it was not eager to add the Palestinian population of the Gaza Strip and the West Bank to its body politic. Palestinian leaders had the authority and credibility to make a compromise agreement that their predecessors had refused to consider. But accommodation and compromise remained only theoretical options. Israeli attachment to the West Bank intensified, while the PLO was carried away by its initial successes to an inflated view of its power and prospects.[13]

By the summer of 1970, it had become clear that the PLO's efforts to organize a popular uprising in the West Bank and the Gaza Strip were unsuccessful. Still more significant, the Arab states' war of attrition against Israel had run its course, and Egypt's president, Gamal Abdel Nasser, responded positively to Secretary of State William Rogers's "initiative" for a cease-fire. The PLO's radical wing fought a rearguard action against what it viewed as capitulation. Western airliners were hijacked to Cairo and Jordan. In Jordan this defiance triggered a final showdown between the Palestinians and the Hashemite regime. For three years, King Hussein had tolerated the gradual erosion of his authority and sovereignty in Jordan by a movement that enjoyed the support of both the Palestinian majority among his own subjects and the larger Arab world. In September 1970, the Palestinians overplayed their hand, humiliating him and his loyalists, but the Jordanian army crushed the Palestinian opposition and expelled the PLO's fighting units from Jordanian territory without incurring significant criticism from Nasser, who had just made his own truce with Israel. A halfhearted Syrian intervention ended ignominiously: Hafez al-Assad, commander of the Syrian air force, refused to commit his planes to what he regarded as a senseless adventure, and without air cover the Syrian armored column invading Jordan fell easy prey to Jordan's small air force and was forced to turn around.

There was more to this episode than a minor military clash between Jordan and Syria. It was also a Soviet-

American conflict by proxy. In the Cold War context, a Soviet client had invaded the territory of an American client, and had apparently been defeated by the latter's armed forces, though it was also deterred by the deployment of Israeli land and air forces. Israel's moves were closely coordinated with the United States, which viewed this coordination as a successful implementation of the Nixon doctrine—resolving a regional crisis with local allies and without American troops. This was the first in a series of exploits by Henry Kissinger that defined his spectacular Middle Eastern diplomacy during the next years.

In Israel a retrospective policy debate followed this episode. Henry Kissinger's chief partner on the Israeli side had been Yitzhak Rabin, who was serving as ambassador to Washington—a preparatory phase in his transition from a military career to a political one. He and the government of Prime Minister Golda Meir as a whole took pride in what they considered a clear demonstration of Israel's strategic value to the United States, its contribution to pragmatism and stability in the region, and the reinforcement of Israel's community of interests with the Hashemite regime in Jordan. Curiously, the government's right-wing critics took exception to this latter point; in their view, Israel should have remained neutral in the Jordanian dispute and allowed the Palestinians to defeat the Hashemite regime and take over the Jordanian government, for they believed that, once the Palestinians had their own state in Jordan, Israel could press its claim to the West Bank. Thus the maxim "Jordan is Palestine."[14]

But this Israeli debate seemed almost academic. The successful conclusion of the Jordanian crisis, the end of the war of attrition, Nasser's subsequent death, and the partnership and intimacy with the United States combined to generate a feeling that the status quo could be indefinitely perpetuated. This, however, came from a false sense of complacency.[15]

The war launched in October 1973 by Egypt and Syria against Israel differed from those of 1948 and 1967. They did not go to war in support of the Palestinians or drift into it in an uncontrolled process of escalation. But the Sinai Peninsula for Egypt and the Golan Heights for Syria were parts of their national territories, and Israel's control of them seemed unbearable. The real driving force that planned and executed the war was Nasser's underestimated successor, Anwar al-Sadat.

Sadat's new policy toward Israel was predicated on his underlying decision to liberalize Egypt's politics and economy and to reorient that nation from a Soviet to an American focus. In order to implement these changes, he had to disengage from the conflict with Israel. His concepts for a diplomatic settlement with Israel were very modest (and very distant from the peace treaty he ended up signing nine years later), but they were unacceptable to Golda Meir in 1971, and he decided to launch a limited war in order to break the deadlock.

Sadat relied on two partners. One was Syria's new ruler, Hafez al-Assad, who seized full power in his country in November 1970 after an internecine debate over Syria's debacle in Jordan two months earlier. Assad, a senior member of the Ba'ath regime since its inception in March 1963, headed its more pragmatic wing. He did not believe in the ill-defined notion of a "popular war of liberation," but advocated cooperation with other Arab states against Israel. When Sadat approached him in 1972, he agreed to join Egypt in a war coalition, though he did not share Sadat's concept of the war as a prelude to negotiations or relish Syria's junior-partner position. Sadat's other partner was the group of conservatively governed, oil-producing Arab states. By the early 1970s, the first signs of the "energy crisis" were visible, and the balance among the oil-producing nations, the international oil companies, and the Western powers was shifting. Sadat knew that in launching war he could rely on the increasing political and economic power of the Gulf Arabs.[16]

The PLO was not part of or privy to these preparations. Having been evicted from Jordan, it was busy building a new territorial base in Lebanon. The weakness of the Lebanese state, the sympathy and support of several factions within Lebanon, and the backing of other Arab governments enabled it to build a "state within a state" there—with virtual control over Palestinian refugee camps in Beirut and in the south, autonomous political and operational headquarters in Beirut, and an extensive infrastructure in southern Lebanon, which it could use as a base of operations against Israel.

1973–77

The October War of 1973 did indeed break the deadlock and opened the way to a lengthy, intermittent effort to convert the potential created by the 1967 Six-Day War into peace negotiations that would settle the Arab-Israeli conflict. The transition from violence to diplomacy was facilitated by the absence of a clear outcome to the war, which ended with Israeli troops on the Egyptian side of the Suez Canal, a hundred kilometers from Cairo, and also in Syrian territory, within artillery range of Damascus to the north. Only forceful intervention by the United States saved Egypt from a total military defeat. But Egypt did effect a successful crossing of the Suez Canal and managed to keep some troops inside the Sinai Peninsula. And Syria, before its troops were pushed back toward Damascus, had overrun the Golan Heights. Due to an intelligence setback caused by political shortsightedness and a bureaucratic mindset, Israel had been caught by surprise, and at first its armed forces performed poorly. Its recovery and subsequent performance were most impressive, but the meaning of the war's early phases could not be forgotten: the large number of casualties, the need for American resupplies, and therefore the collapse of an important element in strategic U.S.-Israeli cooperation—the belief that Israel could hold its own against any Arab coalition so long as the United States deterred the Soviet Union.

Given the war's ambiguous outcome and the danger of resumed hostilities, the chief protagonists sought an accommodation, and their early agreements became the starting points for a new Arab-Israeli diplomacy led and driven by President Richard Nixon and Secretary of State Kissinger, whose sense of urgency derived from several sources: the energy crisis, the quadrupling of oil prices by Iran and the principal Arab oil-producing states (which clearly took advantage of the war to effect a change they had been planning for some time), and the danger of a confrontation with the Soviet Union if war broke out again.

Beyond these immediate considerations, additional forces were at work. The debacle and shock of the early days in the October War disabused many Israelis of the sense of power they had enjoyed ever since their victory in 1967 and paved the way for significant changes in domestic politics and national-security policies. The full extent of this domestic change was manifested only in 1977, when the Labor movement, after fifty years of hegemony in pre-state and independent Israel, lost power to the right-wing Likud alignment. But meanwhile a yearning for peace and a weariness with bloodshed provided public support for the concessions made in foreign policy by Prime Minister Meir and her successor, Yitzhak Rabin, in 1974 and 1975.

The Arab states were buffeted by contradictory forces. The Egyptian and Syrian armies' initial success, and the swelling of Arab economic power and political influence, tilted many Arabs against the notion of a compromise with Israel. These were the years (1973–82) of the "Arab Decade," when the rest of the world sought Arab oil and money and Arabs could reasonably hope that as a result Israel's base of international support might be undermined. Other Arabs were more cautious. If Israel could not be defeated even when caught by surprise, as it had been in 1973, with its military machine out of gear, what was the point of waiting for some prospective opportunity to fight it in the future? From that perspective, there was no value in a long-drawn-out effort to erode Israel's position when significant concessions might be obtained through diplomacy.[17]

After the October War, Sadat completed the move he had begun in 1972, when he expelled the Soviet Union's military advisers from Egypt, and placed his country squarely within the American orbit. Indeed, for Henry Kissinger, his partner in this transition, the Israeli-Arab peace process was not only a mechanism for preventing another war, for directing Arab-Israeli relations on the path of resolution, and for calming the Arab oil-producers, but also part of a strategy designed to facilitate precisely this shift of allegiance. And the success of that strategy was one of the United States' greatest achievements during the Cold War. But Kissinger's effort to apply the same rule to Syria met with only limited success. Assad concluded one agreement with Israel and began negotiating with Washington, but he refused to abandon his pro-Soviet orientation.

Alongside the American mediation, a direct channel of communication between Egypt and Israel was opened after the October War: talks between Generals Abd-ul-Ghani al-Gamasi and Aharon Yariv at Kilometer 101, a site named for its sign marking the distance from Cairo. The talks revealed the potential for reconciliation inherent in the relationship between the two countries, but at the end of the day both preferred to have Washington's mediation. With American help, Egypt and Israel signed a number of agreements that led to a further agreement in January 1974. This stabilized the situation and indicated the direction further peace negotiations could take: it stipulated Israel's withdrawal from the Egyptian mainland and from the banks of the Suez Canal. Egypt thus emerged from the war with its first concrete achievement, while Israel could relish the opportunity to regroup and contemplate its next moves, taking comfort in the notion that a withdrawal from the Suez Canal was a sine qua non for starting a peace process with Egypt. (Israel could also ask itself whether it had been necessary to go through the October War to come to that conclusion.)

Kissinger's mediation efforts and the three accords they yielded—disengagement agreements between Israel and Egypt and then Syria in January and May 1974, and the Israeli-Egyptian interim agreement of September 1975—were referred to at the time as "step-by-step" diplomacy. As this implied, U.S. policy was to aim not for a comprehensive settlement of the Arab-Israeli conflict but for a series of partial, interim agreements. The pessimistic presumption was that a comprehensive, final settlement that met Arab demands and expectations and also addressed Israel's needs and concerns was not feasible under prevailing circumstances. Though almost everyone paid lip service to the idea of a comprehensive settlement by coming to a brief Arab-Israeli peace conference held in Geneva under UN auspices in December 1973, this was an essentially ritualistic affair designed to placate the Soviet Union and Arab nationalist opinion, both of which resented Washington's control of the negotiations and its preference for partial bilateral agreements.[18]

Syria boycotted this conference, but was eager nonetheless to collaborate with the United States in negotiating a disengagement agreement with Israel. It was a protracted and arduous negotiation. Though Syria had fewer bargaining chips than Egypt, it was determined to obtain an equivalent agreement, and Assad bargained hard, reinforcing his diplomacy with a minor war of attrition. The agreement finally reached in May 1974 provided for Israel's withdrawal from the territory it had captured beyond the Golan Heights in October 1973 and from Quneitra, the provincial capital there. Like Sadat, Assad thus managed to win back a slice of the territory his country had lost in 1967. But whereas in the Egyptian case the postwar disengagement agreement was only a first step in a phased process, the Israeli-Syrian agreement of May 1974 had no sequel.

In the early summer of 1974, it was clear that Israel and Egypt were ready for the next stage of their negotiations, but the substantive issues were compounded by a procedural problem. Sadat was willing to defy the Arab nationalist demand for a comprehensive agreement with Israel, but he was not willing to go it alone. Syria had been Egypt's partner until now, but the idea of pairing the two again did not appeal to anyone; Assad had acquired the reputation of being a tough, meticulous negotiator, and the Golan Heights' limited terrain offered limited choices. A short-lived effort was made to bring in Jordan: Kissinger's idea was to offer Jordan a bridgehead in the area of Jericho as a prelude to its getting back the West Bank. To Israel's new prime minister and to the Labor Party as a whole, Jordan was a preferable partner to the PLO in resolving the Palestinian problem, but Rabin was not ready to make a bold move that would address this underlying issue in Israeli politics and public life, for though it might possibly provide a satisfactory solution it would certainly generate bitter controversies. This was not Rabin the mature statesman of the 1990s, but a political novice still, entrusted with ultimate responsibility at a very difficult time. So Rabin rejected Kissinger's initiative. Shortly thereafter, the Arab states, in a consensus formulated in a summit conference at Rabat, formally denied Jordan's claim to the West Bank and recognized the PLO as "the sole legitimate representative of the Palestinian People" and as the rightful claimant to those parts of historic Palestine that Israel might give up in future negotiations.[19]

Given this sequence of events, Egypt decided to go it alone in negotiations with Israel. After nearly a year of arduous work, an interim agreement over the Sinai Peninsula was signed: Egypt regained its oil fields there and the strategic Mitla and Gidi passes; a collateral U.S.-Israeli memorandum of understanding was also signed that advanced the two nations' strategic and diplomatic cooperation still further.

The interim agreement represented the high point of Kissinger's "step-by-step" diplomacy, but it may also have marked its end. At least one additional phase might have been planned in the Sinai, but it was not at all clear that Sadat was able or willing to face an angry Arab chorus led by Syria. Kissinger showed his own ambivalence when he allowed a senior State Department official, Harold Saunders, to state in a congressional hearing in October 1975 that the Palestinian issue was "the core of the problem." If this was indeed the case, there was only a limited value to negotiations that avoided it. In any event, the outbreak of civil war in Lebanon in 1975–76 and the Ford administration's preoccupation with the presidential election in November 1976 resulted in a virtual suspension of Middle Eastern diplomacy.[20]

1977–82

Jimmy Carter's election and the inauguration of his administration in January 1977 began a new phase in Israeli-

Arab relations. President Carter and his team—Secretary
of State Cyrus Vance, National Security Adviser Zbigniew
Brzezinski, and Harold Saunders and William Quandt as
the bureaucratic experts on the Middle East—were motivated by a host of new considerations: an open desire to
distance themselves from their predecessors' policies, a
genuine belief that a final and comprehensive settlement
of the Arab-Israeli conflict could be made, diminished interest in East-West Cold War rivalries and a concurrent
preoccupation with tensions between North and South,
concern about the supply and price of oil, and a religiously
inspired sense of mission. Carter's new Middle Eastern
policy not only reversed Kissinger's, but turned a comprehensive settlement of the Arab-Israeli conflict into a major
goal. His administration's concept of comprehensiveness
meant an international conference, cooperation with the
Soviet Union, and the allocation of significant roles to
Syria and the PLO. Carter made no secret of the fact that,
in line with a Brookings Institution report which inspired
his policies, he believed that Israel should withdraw practically all the way back to its pre-1967 borders and should
allow for the establishment of a Palestinian state, in return
for diplomatic recognition and peace that Israel would obtain from the Arab states.

These views and policies pitted Carter against Prime
Minister Rabin and, after May 1977, his successor, Menachem Begin. But they also confounded President Sadat,
who could not understand why the United States would
want to bring the Soviet Union back to center stage in the
Middle East and relegate Egypt, its newfound ally, to a
role secondary to that of uncooperative Syria. Egypt's and
Israel's concern with these developments led to their

forming a direct channel of communication between them. By means of it, the groundwork was laid for Sadat's historic journey to Jerusalem and for the negotiations that led to the Camp David Accords of September 1978 and to the Egyptian-Israeli peace treaty of March 1979.[21]

Shared exasperation with the policies of the Carter administration certainly helped to start this direct Egyptian-Israeli dialogue, but both parties were also moved by more significant considerations. Sadat wanted, of course, to regain the whole of the Sinai Peninsula. In 1977, he understood that this was a realistic possibility but full peace had to be offered in return. Early in his presidency, Sadat had decided that disengagement from the conflict with Israel was integral to a realignment of Egypt's policies and politics, but he had not thought through a plan and had only a sense of direction, some rudimentary notions, and an understanding of the Egyptians' weariness. By 1977, he had several years' experience, self-confidence gained in the October War and its sequel, and a clearer idea of what had to be done.

In Menachem Begin, Sadat found a surprising, not to say unlikely, yet effective partner. On May 17, 1977, after defeats in previous elections, Begin finally won and became Israel's prime minister, a victory that ended Labor Zionism's hegemony and represented the first genuine transfer of power in Israeli politics. The accession to power of a nationalist right-wing politician was unanimously expected to exacerbate Arab-Israeli relations. But this expectation failed to take account of two significant changes in Israeli politics: as a newcomer, Begin was less constrained by convention than his predecessors had been; and as a nationalist ideologue, he was totally com-

mitted to the idea of the Land of Israel (Eretz Yisrael) yet
not to the Sinai Peninsula—from which, it turned out, he
was willing to offer full withdrawal in order to achieve
peace.

A separate peace was not what Sadat had in mind. The
discrepancy between his and Begin's ideas of what peace
meant produced an early crisis in their direct negotiations
that was resolved by the United States. Washington's initial response to direct Egyptian-Israeli dialogue had been
quite cold, but the president and his team soon understood that, whatever their own hopes, once Egypt and Israel were in direct negotiation, both opportunities and
dangers presented themselves that U.S. policy had to address. The unusual gathering at Camp David was the culmination of a process that made the United States a third,
often dominant partner in the negotiations and introduced
a kind of mediation-cum-arbitration into what had originally been direct give-and-take.

The Camp David Accords turned Arab-Israeli diplomacy into a full-blown effort to achieve peace. By extending diplomatic recognition to Israel, signing a peace treaty
with it, and establishing normal relations with it, Sadat and
Egypt violated a taboo that an Arab consensus had strictly
enforced for more than three decades. There were two
parts to the Camp David Accords—an Israeli-Egyptian
agreement terminating the bilateral dispute between
them, and a framework laying down the principles for resolving Israel's conflict over the Palestinians and its disputes with other Arab neighbors. But the two parts were
not of equal importance. Begin and Sadat were primarily
interested in their bilateral agreement, and both leaders
saw to its strict implementation. Indeed, this was how the

Arab world perceived the agreements: as Sadat's having broken ranks and made a separate peace with Israel. He was denounced and vilified, Egypt was ousted from the Arab League, and most Arab states severed diplomatic relations with Cairo.[22]

Sadat reacted angrily to this criticism. He viewed himself not as a traitor to the Arab cause but as a pathfinder showing the Arab world the only course open to it for regaining territories lost in 1967. When Assad and other critics accused him of being a careless and ineffective negotiator, he retorted that they were small-minded men who focused on minor details and failed to see the overall picture. He kept saying that his loudest critics would end up following in his footsteps—a judgment that was vindicated posthumously.

As for Begin, he exploited part of the potential created in June 1967 to resolve the "conflict of 1948" on the Egyptian front. His far-reaching achievement—Israel's peace agreement with Egypt—was the most significant breakthrough in Arab-Israeli relations to date, but the price was commensurate. Sadat was willing to offer Israel full peace and generous security arrangements in the Sinai, but he insisted on regaining the whole territory, every last square inch. By agreeing to this, Begin not only conceded the whole of the Sinai but established a precedent (in fact explicitly): full withdrawal for full peace.

Furthermore, if Begin expected Sadat to treat the Palestinian dimension of the agreement as a mere formality and allow Israel a free hand in the West Bank, he misunderstood. In the Israeli-Egyptian negotiation of 1977–78 Sadat had pressed for recognition of the Palestinians' "national rights." Begin, worried by the potential ramifications of this abstract principle, had put forth his autonomy plan, to which Sadat had reacted coldly. But once it was agreed on, Egypt pressed hard for a liberal interpretation of "full autonomy" for the Palestinians. A deadlock was reached on this issue, and relations between Israel and Egypt soured.

The failure to implement the Palestinian component of the Egyptian-Israeli peace treaty allowed Sadat and his successors a convenient justification for keeping bilateral relations between the two countries at a low level, or, as it came to be known, for "the cold peace." Egypt has kept its principal commitments to Israel (full diplomatic relations, a security regime in the Sinai, free access to Egypt for all Israeli tourists) but has imposed severe restrictions on the development of normal relations in the economic and cultural spheres and has continued its political and diplomatic rivalry. Thus the collapse of the "autonomy negotiations" in 1980, which seemed at the time only a temporary setback, was perpetuated over the next decade, and several events and developments helped: Jimmy Carter's loss in his re-election campaign, Sadat's assassination, the Lebanon war, the Iran-Iraq war, the changes in the PLO's standing and position, and new trends in Israeli politics.

1982–91

There were two aims to the war Israel launched in Lebanon in June 1982. One was to resolve once and for all the host of problems presented by the collapse of the

Lebanese state in the civil war of 1975–76. But on another
level, the war's plan reflected a much more ambitious effort to bring about a sweeping change in the whole region.
As Ariel Sharon, architect of the war, saw it, Israel could
transform its regional position by inflicting serious blows
on Syria and the PLO and by installing a friendly regime
in Lebanon. This flawed plan failed on both levels. Israel's
regional position was not transformed, and the general
challenge of the Lebanese problems has only continued.
The confrontation with the PLO has been replaced by a
confrontation with the Shi'ite community and two Shi'ite
militias—Amal and, subsequently, Hizballah. The latter
is a political movement and also a militia and terrorist
organization operated directly from Teheran. During and
after the conflict with Israel and the United States in
1982–84, Syria consolidated and further institutionalized
its hegemony in Lebanon; as part of its strategic alliance
with Iran, Syria affords it access to the Shi'ite community
in Lebanon and acquiesces in its control of Hizballah,
though it imposes limits on its activities.[23]

The Islamic revolution in Iran in 1979 that brought the
Ayatollah Khomeini and his fundamentalist regime to
power was a cardinal event in the modern history of the
Middle East. For Israel, it put an end to a vital relationship the nation had established in prior years with the
Shah of Iran, and placed Iran's considerable potential at
the service of the Arab world's radical wing. Ever since,
the Islamic Republic of Iran has agitated against Israel
and against the notion of Arab-Israeli reconciliation, has
used its extensive networks in the Middle East and other
parts of the world for anti-Israeli terrorist activities, and

has introduced new elements, like suicide bombings, into the Shi'ite-Lebanese and Palestinian conflicts with Israel. But at first these negative effects were mitigated by other developments. The fall of the Shah and the rise of the Ayatollahs also upset a delicate balance of power in the Persian Gulf region. It had always been difficult to maintain stability when several rich but weak states, and two wealthy powerful states—one a conservative monarchy and the other a radical republic—were all in the act. When the conservative monarchy in Iran was taken over by revolutionary clerics the balance became impossible, and indeed Iraq launched a war against Iran that lasted nearly eight years. The war gave the weaker Arab states in the Gulf region a breathing spell, but inevitably the end of the Iran-Iraq war in 1988 shifted the tension elsewhere; this happened in 1990.

While all this was going on, a substantial change occurred in the agenda and priorities of the conservative oil-producing states of the Arabian Peninsula. In the 1960s and 1970s, they had been genuinely concerned about the Arab-Israeli conflict and its radicalizing effect on their own polities; in the 1980s, different dangers were emanating from Iran and Iraq, which meant a change of attitude toward the conflict with Israel, as well as the peace process. The former was dwarfed by existential threats posed by Iran and Iraq; and peace between Egypt and Israel—the object of sharp criticism in 1978–79—now seemed more positive, stabilizing the western part of the region and freeing Egypt's armed forces to defend the Arabian Peninsula against the two radical republics. This change of perspective facilitated a reconciliation between

Egypt and the other nations of the Arab world and enabled Sadat's successor to join them without having to give
up the new relationship with Israel.[24]

At the same time, American leadership during Ronald
Reagan's eight years in the White House lacked the drive,
conviction, and determination that his two predecessors
(and successor) displayed vis-à-vis the Middle East. Reagan seemed warmly disposed toward Israel, but he lacked
any emotional commitment to the Camp David Accords,
his rival's great achievement, and also lacked the messianic
zeal that drove the Carter administration's quest to bring
peace to the Middle East. Reagan's administration was
damaged badly by a series of negative experiences in the
Middle East—the crisis in Lebanon, the virtual rejection
of his September 1982 "Reagan Plan," the Iran-Contra
affair—and turned its foreign-policy efforts elsewhere,
mostly to the great struggle against the Soviet Union. Secretary of State George Shultz did invest time and ingenu-
ity in his efforts to revive the Arab-Israeli peace process,
notably in 1987 and 1988, but drive and muscle were lack-
ing. The effort to make an Israeli-Jordanian agreement
(the London Agreement of 1987) and to turn the PLO
into an acceptable partner (in 1988) failed.

The debacle in Lebanon was the beginning of the end
of the Begin era in Israeli politics, but the Likud alignment's decline was not matched by a return to Labor as-
cendancy. The elections of 1984 and 1988 produced six
years of power-sharing under two versions of national-
unity governments: the first gave a domestic political
base for an (almost complete) Israeli withdrawal from
Lebanon, but the Labor leader Shimon Peres's effort
to revive the peace process, whether as prime minister

(1984–86) or as foreign minister (1986–88), were to no avail; then Labor brought down the second national-unity government in 1990, when it believed that Likud was not responding to Secretary of State James Baker's efforts to restart the peace process.

At the core of the Likud-Labor disagreement were two conflicting approaches to an Israeli-Arab, or Israeli-Palestinian, settlement. Tactically, these differences were translated into a debate over the acceptability of various Palestinian negotiators and their affiliations to the PLO. Likud's opposition to the PLO was absolute. The Labor Party's leaders also refused to accept the organization as a legitimate negotiating partner, but were willing to accept certain Palestinian negotiators whose relationship with the PLO was not direct or explicit. Still, at the end, it was Likud and its right-wing allies that were able to form a new government, and the Labor Party went back to the opposition.

Not every twist and turn in Israeli politics during the 1980s derived from the Likud-Labor rivalry and their respective ideologies, but a significant pattern could be identified: between 1977 and 1992 Israel was governed for thirteen years by a Likud prime minister and for only two years by a Labor prime minister. This shows the preeminence, however slight, of conservative nationalist forces in the Israeli body politic. Thus it was a right-wing Israeli government that confronted the massive changes of the early 1990s.[25]

On the other side, three forces had contended since 1967 to be the effective and legitimate representation of the Palestinian cause: the PLO, Jordan, and ill-defined local forces in the West Bank and the Gaza Strip. The PLO was dealt a severe blow in the Lebanon war of 1982; the subsequent removal of its headquarters and fighting forces to Tunis and to the Yemen was a severe handicap. But there was no one else to take advantage of its predicament. The failed London Agreement of 1987 was the last time an effort was made to have Jordan be Israel's principal partner in resolving the Palestinian issue, but it failed before its feasibility could be tested.

When the Palestinian uprising, the *intifada*, broke out spontaneously in 1987, it was sustained by individuals and groups that were not part of the PLO's hierarchy, yet the political capital it generated was ultimately captured by the PLO, though the road it traveled was far from straight: first acceptance of a formula for a two-state solution in 1988, then the establishment of a dialogue with the United States, the breakdown of that dialogue after the PLO's fresh drift into sponsorship of terrorism, and misguided support of Saddam Hussein's Iraq after his invasion of Kuwait.

THE TURNING POINT OF THE
MADRID CONFERENCE

The Madrid Conference of October 1991 finally placed the Arab-Israeli peace process on a qualitatively different footing. This first sustained effort by the international community to resolve the old conflict[26] was the product of three principal developments.

First, the decline and dissolution of the Soviet Union put an end to the Cold War's deleterious effects on Arab-

Israeli issues. It left the United States as the sole power capable of exercising influence for settlement, while the Soviet Union's Arab clients lost their chief source of aid for their subsidized weapon systems. Rulers like Syria's Hafez al-Assad found themselves looking for substitutes, seeking out the United States, and dealing with the repercussions of the fall of Eastern European dictators. Israel, on the other hand, was a clear beneficiary. Soviet and Eastern-bloc hostility was replaced by normal (in several cases friendly) relations.

Also, the arrival in Israel of nearly a million immigrants from the former Soviet Union had a very significant substantive and psychological effect on the Arab-Israeli balance. In absolute terms the addition of a million Jews to the Arab-Israeli demographic equation may not seem very impressive. Israel now has 5 million Jewish and 1 million Arab (or Palestinian) citizens; also, more than 2 million Palestinians live in the West Bank and the Gaza Strip. The overall number of Palestinians is estimated at about 7 million (and the total population of the Arab world at more than 200 million). Still, the disappearance of the radical Arabs' principal mainstay and the influx of 1 million Jews to Israel sufficed to persuade many Arabs that time was not necessarily on their side.

Second, the United States, having already benefited from the Soviet Union's decline, saw its position and standing in the Middle East rise to a new level after the world witnessed its willingness and ability to field half a million soldiers and build an international coalition for the liberation of Kuwait and the defense of Saudi Arabia. The war weakened Arab radicals and the PLO. (The PLO leaders, aware of their diminished position, consented to being demoted, as it were, to only indirect representation at the Madrid Conference.) The United States also emerged from the war determined to take advantage of its enhanced influence and prestige in order to seek a comprehensive solution to the Arab-Israeli conflict. The Bush administration saw this as a necessary prerequisite for stability and for a reorganized Middle East. It also believed, given Iraq's launching of Scud missiles against Israel in the Gulf War, that the danger that weapons of mass destruction would be used in future wars was more acute. A political settlement was vital.

Third, the Palestinians' uprising in the West Bank and in Gaza beginning in late 1987, the *intifada*, had a long and profound effect on the Israeli public. Ever since the 1967 war twenty years before, Palestinians had failed to devise an effective strategy for their struggle against Israel, and whenever Israeli society weighed the costs of keeping the status quo or working out a new compromise, the balance had tilted toward maintaining the status quo. But in 1988, a significant body of opinion in Israel was no longer willing to pay the costs of a perpetuated status quo. It is impossible to understand Yitzhak Shamir's acceptance of the "Madrid framework" or the Labor Party's victory in the 1992 elections without understanding the effect of this change.

It took several months of hard work by Secretary of State James Baker, including nine trips to the Middle East, to build upon these developments and put together the formula for convening an international conference. A compromise had to be worked out between Arab and Israeli points of departure. As I have already noted, a weakened PLO had to give up hopes for direct participation in the conference and in ensuing negotiations; Syria, which had hoped for years for significant roles for the Soviet Union and the UN, one single Arab delegation, and continuous negotiation thereafter, finally agreed to a process co-sponsored by the Soviet Union but dominated by the United States, and on comparatively loose coordination among four Arab-Israeli negotiating tracks. Israel accepted the notion of an international conference and was willing to turn a blind eye to the Palestinian delegation's real source of authority.

The final texts of the letter of invitation to the Madrid Conference and of the different letters of assurance given by the United States to the different participants clearly expressed the bitter arguments over these principles and terms, and the nature of the compromise solutions finally worked out by Secretary Baker and his team. Thus the phrase "territories for peace" was not included in the text of the letter of initiation to the Madrid Conference or in the specific letter of assurances sent to Israel, but it was mentioned in the letters of assurance addressed to the Arab invitees. For Shamir's government, the fact that the Palestinians formally had no separate representation but were present only as part of a Jordanian-Palestinian delegation was an achievement.

Another Baker achievement (and Syrian concession) was the formation of a second, multilateral negotiation to supplement the bilateral one. Working groups were established to focus on five regional issues: water, refugees, arms control and regional security, environment, and economic cooperation. The original idea was to generate discussion of how to achieve regional cooperation on these matters and paint visions of a better future, which would facilitate the concessions that all the parties on the bilateral track would have to make. This plan proved to be particularly fruitful, even though Syria and Lebanon refused to join these multilateral talks. It enabled a group of states from outside the region to take an active part in the peace process, bringing in Arab states from the Gulf, the Arabian Peninsula, and North Africa, and accelerating Arab-Israeli normalization.

At the Madrid Conference, where for the first time the international community, led by the United States, committed itself to a sustained effort to resolve the Arab-Israeli conflict, a framework and a set of rules were accepted by all parties. As we have seen, a measure of ambiguity was maintained, but the Madrid formula was more explicit than, say, Security Council Resolution 242 had been. Diplomatic ambiguity and various protestations notwithstanding, it was clear that Israel wanted full peace with the Arabs, and the Arabs wanted massive territorial concessions. "Territories for peace" of course did not mean "all of Israel's occupied territories for peace," but the phrase was nonetheless unacceptable even to Shamir's government, although its leaders had come to understand that their advocacy of "peace for peace" was unrealistic.

The Madrid formula also showed that a new balance had been struck between the Palestinian and larger Arab components of the conflict. Earlier, choices had to be made in practice between Palestinians and the Arab states. The Geneva Conference and Kissinger's "step-by-step" diplomacy were both predicated on a conscious policy to bypass the Palestinians and the Palestinian issue. President Carter's attempt to put the PLO and the Palestinian issue at the center of a comprehensive settlement was an important reason for its failure. True, the Camp David Accords and the Egyptian-Israeli peace treaty incorporated the notion of interim or transitional Palestinian self-government, but this remained a dead letter. The Bush administration had, prior to the Gulf crisis, focused exclusively on the issue of Palestinian autonomy. But in 1991, the idea of dealing simultaneously with the Palestinians *and* with the Arab states was one of the keys to Jim Baker's success.

Yet the forces that produced the Madrid successes could not take them beyond a certain point. The opening conference was impressive, but during the next nine months and five rounds of negotiations in Washington, no progress was made. It was clear from the outset that a breakthrough could happen only on the Syrian or the Palestinian track, that progress with Jordan and Lebanon would have to come later. However, the Syrian and Palestinian protagonists were unwilling to make the concessions needed for progress, let alone for a breakthrough. The Bush administration, having invested a great deal of effort and political capital in Madrid, was not ready for the cost and pain entailed in goading the parties on; it was openly critical of Shamir and his government and was willing to wait for the Israeli elections of June 1992, hoping that a Labor victory would lead to change.

MADRID AND OSLO:
YEARS OF HOPE

As the century draws to a close, the four-year period from June 1992 to May 1996, shrouded as it is by both nostalgia and controversy, looms ever more distinctly as a notably significant chapter in the evolution of Arab-Israeli relations. A hospitable regional and international environment, the newly formed Madrid framework, American leadership and support, and, above all, the determination of two Israeli prime ministers to move toward peace and several Arab partners' positive response to this, produced the most ambitious and sustained effort yet to settle the Arab-Israeli conflict.[1] These ambitions endowed the period with significance, and a number of important breakthroughs changed the contours of Arab-Israeli relations; these produced negative reactions, though, and underlined the limits to achieving a notion of peace that would be acceptable to both Arabs and Israelis.

The term "peace process" is often used rather loosely, but in those years it had a very concrete meaning: four formal tracks of bilateral negotiations supplemented by discreet informal ones, five working multilateral groups, a concerted international effort to give financial and economic support to Arab peace-makers, and two economic conferences (in Casablanca and Amman). These led to the Oslo Agreement between Israel and the PLO, a peace treaty between Israel and Jordan, semi-diplomatic relations established between Israel and four other Arab states, a significant degree of less formal Israeli-Arab normalization, and a widespread sense that the Arab-Israeli conflict was finally on the way to reconciliation and resolution.

Yet the negative reaction to the same set of developments was hardly less significant.[2] Palestinian opponents of the peace process, some of them encouraged and supported by Iran, conducted a terrorist campaign designed to undermine it. Radical Israeli opponents of their government's peace policies perpetrated and condoned a massacre of Palestinian worshippers at the Tomb of the Patriarchs in Hebron in February 1994 and, separately, the assassination of Prime Minister Rabin in November 1995. Violent conflict continued along the Israeli-Lebanese border between Israel and Hizballah, exacting a high toll of casualties on both sides and culminating in Katyusha rocket attacks on northern Israel and two large-scale Israeli military operations in Lebanon. This conflict in Lebanon had local causes, but it should be seen in the context of Iran's effort to undermine the peace process, and of the failure to reach an agreement between Israel and Syria. The peace process was not well received by large segments of public opinion in the Arab world and was bitterly criticized and rejected by the Arab intelligentsia. In Israel it was pursued by a government that relied on a very slim majority, and opposition rose to the agreement made with the PLO and to the agreement contemplated with Syria. This culminated in the assassination of Rabin and the subsequent election of Benjamin (Binyamin, in Hebrew) Netanyahu, who promised to respect the agreements made by his predecessors but also to shift the peace process to an entirely different premise.

The progress made during 1992–96 had one additional and unanticipated effect. Israelis and Arabs had been familiar for some fifteen years with the benefits and limitations of the separate peace between Egypt and Israel, but notions of a comprehensive Arab-Israeli peace remained remote and abstract. The peace process of 1992–96 brought it close and made it more palpable; it showed both sides how limited the concept of peace was that would be acceptable to their societies and political systems.

It may seem odd that the period should be defined by two Israeli elections. But the fact of the matter is that, in the configuration that determined the ebb and flow of the peace process, Yitzhak Rabin's electoral victory in June 1992 marked the beginning of a new chapter, and Benjamin Netanyahu's triumph in 1996 brought it to an end. The 1992–96 peace process unfolded through four distinct phases: from the Israeli elections of June 1992 to the signing of the Oslo Accords in September 1993; from then to the signing of the Israeli-Jordanian peace treaty in October 1994; from then to Rabin's assassination in Novem-

ber 1995; and from then to the Israeli elections of May
1996.

THE ROAD TO OSLO

Yitzhak Rabin's electoral victory in June 1992 was univer-
sally interpreted as the first step in a revived peace
process, and Rabin himself stated clearly that he could
produce an agreement on Palestinian self-rule within nine
months. But neither Rabin nor his eventual partner,
Yasser Arafat, envisaged himself signing an agreement like
the Oslo Accords in a festive ceremony in Washington
fourteen months later. And yet both leaders, in their different styles and within their different environments, ad-
justed and made new choices.

Rabin arrived in the prime minister's office in Jerusalem
in July 1992 as a mature, experienced, and authoritative
political leader. Fifteen years after his earlier resignation,
he had eradicated the memories of that episode and, more
broadly, of his rocky first tenure (1974–77), and now he
projected the image of a confident senior leader, Israel's
ultimate authority on matters of national security, a direct
and trustworthy man, a political leader who was a reluctant politician.[3]

Rabin won twice in 1992. In February, having failed in
earlier challenges, he defeated Shimon Peres in the Labor
Party's primaries and became the party's leader and its
candidate for the premiership. He had finally succeeded
in persuading not only the rank and file but part of the
party apparatus that he alone could defeat Shamir and the

Likud and could return Labor to power. The conventional wisdom in Israeli politics was that Israeli voters had shifted to the right, that they thought Peres was too dovish. Only Rabin, it was felt, identified as he was with national security and more centrist policies, could attract swing votes in the center of the Israeli political spectrum. So Labor's campaign in the subsequent general elections presumed that, though a significant number of voters might be ready to switch their votes away from the Likud, they remained reluctant to cast them for Labor. Accordingly, it focused on the candidate and not on the party. Rabin hammered away on two principal issues: Shamir's inability to move the Madrid peace process forward, and his mismanagement of Israel's relationship with the United States, as evidenced by the manifest tension between his government and the Bush administration. Rabin promised that if elected he would galvanize the peace process and argued that an agreement to give the Palestinians some kind of autonomy could be reached within nine months. (A settlement with Syria did not seem realistic to Rabin at the time, and was not a real issue.)

Rabin won, but only barely so. An analysis of the voting figures in June 1992 shows that the Israeli body politic remained evenly divided between right and left, and that in fact the right received several thousand more votes than the rival bloc but ended up with a slightly smaller representation in the Knesset. Rabin formed a coalition with the left-wing Meretz and with Shas, the latter being an unusual combination of an ultra-Orthodox party and a grass-roots movement of Israelis of North African extraction.

The key term in the new government's agenda was "a

change of national priorities." Rabin, who did not believe that a comprehensive Arab-Israeli peace was likely in the near future, was ready to offer concessions in order to reach an accommodation with the Arabs, but not to return to the 1967 borders. Nor did he believe in simultaneous negotiation with Israel's four Arab protagonists, in which the Arab position would be dictated by the most radical Arab party while Israel would have to make simultaneous concessions on several fronts. Rabin preferred a gradual approach, and in the meantime Israel's domestic, regional, and international positions could be improved.

As minister of defense only a few years before, Rabin had conducted Israel's campaign against the *intifada* sternly and severely, but its lessons were not lost on him. He knew that the cost of holding on indefinitely to the West Bank and Gaza had become prohibitive. An ultimately futile effort was diverting too many resources to the West Bank from Israel proper and exacerbating Israel's relationship with the rest of the world, most significantly with the United States. For Israel's new prime minister it was essential that peace negotiations begin again, that good relations be restored with the United States, that Israel obtain the $10 billion in loan guarantees which the Americans were willing to underwrite and invest them in expanding the economy and strengthening the infrastructure. Israel needed not only to absorb its new immigrants from the former Soviet Union but to prepare for the future.

Yet Rabin was not enamored of the format established in Madrid. Simultaneous formal negotiations with four Arab delegations were not likely to lead to the kind of breakthrough with the Palestinians or Syrians that he wanted. (Lebanon and Jordan could not be counted on to act first, since Lebanon was subordinate to Syria, and Jordan would need the legitimacy of a prior Syrian or Palestinian agreement.) But for the time being, he saw no reason to insist on a different format. His initial preference was to move first on the Palestinian track. In 1989–90, he had cooperated with Secretary Baker in trying to start an Israeli-Palestinian negotiation; given what he knew from that experience, his own readiness, and Arafat's diminished stature, he thought an agreement on self-rule could be reached within nine months: the Palestinian negotiators would be ones who were acceptable to the PLO but not representing it directly. Such an agreement would not, of course, solve the Palestinian problem, but it would take the edge off the confrontations, move people on to a course of accommodation, open up the larger peace process, and improve Israel's international standing.

Yet there were significant advantages to predicating the peace process on an early agreement with Syria, a powerful state ruled by an authoritative government, in contrast to the fragmented Palestinians. Hafez al-Assad was difficult to negotiate with, but Israel's experience showed that once he made an agreement he kept it. An agreement with Syria would also resolve Israel's problems in Lebanon, encourage Jordan to seek agreement, and thus strengthen Israel's hand with the Palestinians. Still, Syria was likely to insist on discussing only a final settlement, to settle on nothing short of Israel's full withdrawal from Syrian territory, and to offer less than what Israel had in mind.

Rabin's original preferences were modified during Secretary Baker's final trip to the Middle East in July 1992. Baker went first to Damascus and then, in Jerusalem, impressed Rabin both with his account of Assad's willingness to come to a genuine peace agreement and with the Bush administration's willingness to help in reaching it. From that point on, Prime Minister Rabin realized that the only practical course open was to forget about the comparative advantages of this or that possible breakthrough and explore instead the possibilities afforded by the new circumstances.[4]

To begin with, the new government decided to cease building new settlements for Jews on the West Bank. To Syria it offered an implicit acceptance of the principle of withdrawal as a component in a prospective settlement. The effect of these small but significant gestures was felt during the sixth session of talks held in Washington from August 24 to September 2. The format did not change, but those sessions were marked by a new atmosphere, and substantive progress was made.

Syria responded to Israel's opening gambit by presenting, on September 1, 1992, a draft of a proposed Declaration of Principles about a Syrian-Israeli peace agreement. The concepts underlying this draft and the positions presented in it were all totally unacceptable to Israel, but, in contrast to Israeli-Syrian relations during the previous four rounds of Washington talks—an acrimonious dialogue of the deaf—its very presentation and its mention of a Syrian-Israeli peace agreement were emblematic of significant changes.

By the end of 1992, this good momentum had been all but dissipated. The Palestinian delegation to the talks in Washington, operating under instructions from the PLO leaders in Tunis, and the Israeli delegation were at cross-purposes. (The Palestinian delegation, composed of residents of the West Bank and the Gaza Strip, was headed by a distinguished Palestinian nationalist, Dr. Haidar Abdul Shafi from Gaza, but it was common knowledge that for all intents and purposes the group was controlled and monitored by the PLO leaders in Tunis.) And the Israelis and Syrians were bogged down by Syria's insistence on Israel's commitment to a full withdrawal from the Golan Heights as a precondition to any further give-and-take. In December, Israel cracked down on the radical Islamic opposition in territory under its direct control by deporting some four hundred members of Hamas, the Islamic Resistance movement, to Lebanon. The Arab parties at the Washington talks knew very well that Hamas was challenging them, too, but they responded to Israel's move by suspending their participation in the negotiations.

What were the principal forces that were slowing down or stalling the hoped-for peace?

One was the continued discrepancy between Israeli and Arab outlooks. Syria tried hard to rally the four Arab negotiating parties, and indeed the larger Arab world, behind its own concept of a prospective settlement with Israel and of the procedural aspects in the negotiations. Assad was determined to maximize Arab coordination and to seek a comprehensive settlement or an approximation of one. When, in late July 1992, the Arab foreign ministers were invited to Damascus to formulate their strategy in the aftermath of the Israeli elections and in anticipation of the sixth round of the Washington talks, their joint statement of July 25 alluded to some flexibility (the term "peace agreement" was used for the first time), but it also foreshadowed Syria's and the PLO's opposition to the main thrust of Israel's peace policies. The statement noted approvingly the new Israeli government's "relative change in tone and approach" but criticized its failure to declare "its commitment to the basic principles of comprehensive, just and lasting peace in the region through full implementation of Security Council Resolutions 242 and 338 and the principle of the return of all occupied Arab land, including Jerusalem, in return for peace." The foreign ministers "emphasized anew the . . . principles and elements on which the peace process is based." This meant, overall, a "commitment to the objective of comprehensive peace in the region." But the foreign ministers also pledged to "respect and ensure the Palestinian people's right to self-determination and set up their independent state on their national soil"; they stressed "the linkage between the transitional and final stages in the Palestinian track," and pledged to work to eliminate not only "the obstacles that block completing the Palestinian representation to include the inhabitants of Jerusalem and the diaspora," but also the obstacles to "PLO participation in an official manner in the peace process." They also insisted on "the illegitimacy of all forms of Israeli settlement" and called for a "comprehensive solution in all fronts and in all tracks . . . rejecting any attempt to fragment and deal with each party individually."[5]

During the next few months, Syria and the PLO were in fact successful in upholding these principles. The PLO was, indeed, concerned to obtain formal legitimacy for itself in the peace process and to block any interim agreement that was not linked to a final arrangement that met Palestinian nationalism's basic expectations. It made sure that no progress was made in Washington so long as these two principal goals were not met. And a genuine progress between Syria and Israel was totally overshadowed by Assad's insistence on Israeli commitment to a full withdrawal from the Golan Heights. Outside the conference room, Assad objected to any informal, discreet contacts with Israeli diplomats, refused to engage in public diplomacy, and declined to exercise a restraining influence on Hizballah's activities in and from Lebanon.

A second difficulty concerned political developments within the United States. The revival of the "Madrid process" in the summer of 1992 coincided with the diminishing diplomatic effectiveness of the Bush administration. Shortly after Secretary Baker's trip to the Middle East in July, President Bush asked him to leave the Department of State and move to the White House as his chief of staff: it was a desperate effort to salvage Bush's ailing campaign for re-election. Dennis Ross, Baker's chief aide in Israeli-Arab matters, went along with him. Deputy Secretary Lawrence Eagleburger was appointed acting secretary of state. Eagleburger was an authoritative diplomat and policy-maker and he had at his disposal an experienced "peace team," but the reality and perception of a waning presidency undermined his effectiveness. Hafez al-Assad, for one, went on participating in the talks as much to build a new relationship with the Americans as to arrive at a settlement with Israel and regain the Golan Heights. But from his perspective there was no sense in offering concessions to a president whose future prospects appeared increasingly uncertain or, later, after Clinton had defeated Bush, of making concessions in anticipation of working with a new president about whom Assad knew practically nothing. This transitional phase ended only in February 1993, when Bill Clinton's new administration signaled its assignment of high priority to the Arab-Israeli peace process.

A third difficulty was the direct challenge presented by the radical Islamic opponents of peace with Israel. Hamas and the smaller Islamic Jihad were inspired by several sources: opposition to the very notion of a peaceful settlement with Israel, a more specific opposition to the "Madrid process," opposition to and criticism of Yasser Arafat and his team, and Iranian encouragement. The actions of Hamas, the more active and effective of the two, were shaped by a terribly effective logic—violence and terrorism against Israeli targets would undermine the Israeli people's support for peace and would force Israeli counteractions that would disrupt it.[6] And, indeed, by stepping up its deadly activity—Hamas killed three Israeli soldiers in the Gaza Strip on December 7 and an Israeli border-police officer was abducted and murdered on December 13—Hamas provoked Rabin to his radical effort to emasculate, if not destroy, the Hamas infrastructure in the West Bank and the Gaza Strip: the deportation of some four hundred Hamas activists to Lebanon.

When Warren Christopher, the new secretary of state, went to the Middle East in February 1993, this marked the revival of the peace process, which by April was fully back on track. Rabin had his first working visit to the Clinton administration in March, and the Washington talks were resumed in April. Rabin's visit to Washington was especially important, for it laid the foundation for a warm personal relationship between Clinton and Rabin and for a close working relationship between their governments.

But progress was clearly neither smooth nor linear. Rabin completed his work in Washington but had to cut short his visit to the United States because of a wave of terrorist knifing attacks in Tel Aviv.

Coherence and clarity marked the architecture of the new American administration's Middle Eastern policies: a "dual containment" of Iraq and Iran in the east and pursuit of Arab-Israeli peace in the west, two mutually reinforcing policy prongs. By cultivating an Arab-Israeli peace, Washington hoped it would be easy for its conservative Arab allies to support "dual containment," and fostering Israeli-Syrian and Israeli-Palestinian reconciliation should diminish the ability of Iran and other fundamentalist Muslim states to agitate and subvert.[7]

The administration also believed that this Middle Eastern policy had an unusual asset: an authoritative Israeli prime minister who was determined by his own choice to move toward peace and who was ready to offer indispensable concessions. During the previous twenty years, the United States and Israel had cooperated for much of the time, but as a rule American presidents and secretaries of state had to extract concessions from reluctant Israeli prime ministers (including Rabin himself during his first tenure). Here was a unique opportunity.

In their discussions with Rabin in March, Clinton and his team were quite explicit about their preference for effecting the first breakthrough on the Israeli-Syrian track, which seemed eminently feasible given Rabin's willingness to offer significant (though still not specific) territorial concession and assuming Assad's willingness to make peace. They believed Assad could deliver an agreement he would sign, and considered that an Israeli-Syrian peace could be a prelude to an American-Syrian rapprochement; this would detach Syria from Iran's sphere of influence as it were, and be the key to a desirable realignment in the Middle East. Rabin was responsive to this view, but he reminded the Americans that from Israel's point of view a breakthrough would be welcome on either track.

In April, the State Department official in charge of the peace process, Edward Djerijian, was dispatched on a secret mission to President Assad. He bore a letter from President Clinton that was intended to persuade him to open additional discreet channels to Israel and to adopt a bolder, more forthcoming approach in the negotiations. Djerijian's mission, then a second letter from Clinton, a meeting in Vienna between Secretary Christopher and Foreign Minister Shara, and further work between the Israeli and Syrian delegations in Washington all failed to produce results. Nor did U.S. diplomacy succeed in helping the Israeli and Palestinian delegations. Israeli diplomacy, resorting to unorthodox methods, only produced a final breakthrough on this track by means of secret bilateral negotiations that went on in Oslo for several months.

The Oslo talks began, like several similar informal and unauthorized Israeli and Palestinian dialogues, in January 1993. On the Israeli side it had the sponsorship of Deputy Foreign Minister Yossi Beilin, who operated through two of his academic protégés. Beilin took his time before briefing his superior, Foreign Minister Shimon Peres, about these talks, and Peres took his time in reporting to the prime minister.[8]

Rabin's response was complex. He himself was not enamored of the Madrid format and had lost faith in the formal negotiations in Washington. He had authorized some of his own confidants to deal indirectly with the PLO, and in March 1993, during his visit to Washington, had agreed to have Faysal Husseini, the most prominent Palestinian leader in East Jerusalem, join the Palestinian delegation to the Washington talks. Husseini was known to have close ties with the PLO, and his participation in the talks could conceivably be construed as a crack in Israel's adamant claim that Jerusalem's status as an Israeli city was not negotiable. This latter point was finessed by the admittedly weak argument, familiar since 1989, that since Husseini had a West Bank address he could be regarded as a West Banker and not necessarily a Jerusalemite. And as for the PLO connection, Rabin felt that the pretense of dealing with presumably independent local leaders was wearing thin. Husseini was an authentic local leader, whatever his affiliation with the PLO, and his participation in the Washington talks was a last-ditch effort to see whether there was any value to dealing with local leaders by bypassing the PLO. In retrospect, it is clear that Rabin was not really surprised to discover that Husseini, too, received his marching orders from Tunis. For him, the whole episode was a transition to the ensuing negotiation with the PLO.

So, in May 1993, Rabin agreed to formalize and elevate the status of the Oslo talks and dispatched the director general of the Foreign Ministry, Uri Savir, to head the Israeli team there. Rabin's concession was dual: he agreed in fact to negotiate with the PLO, an organization he had until recently demonized, and he assigned the principal work in this negotiation to Shimon Peres and his team. The original division of labor in Rabin's government had reflected the lingering rivalry between the prime minister and the man he had defeated in the party primaries just five months earlier: Rabin had taken charge of the four tracks of bilateral negotiations with the Arabs, while Peres was left with the five working groups in the multilateral talks. Now Rabin was altering the internal balance in his government, but he regarded this as a secondary issue compared with the prospect of a breakthrough with the Palestinian nationalists.[9]

The Oslo negotiations continued into early August. The Palestinian delegation, composed of Abu Alaa (or Ahmad Quray), a senior member of the PLO hierarchy, and two associates, at Israel's insistence provided ample proof that they were valid and effective PLO representatives. On the Israeli side Savir was reinforced by Joel Singer, a retired international lawyer with the Israeli Defense Force. Rabin kept his own close aides and the defense establishment in the dark, and Singer's participation in addition to his own overseeing of the negotiations was intended to ensure that security issues would be covered. By early August, the broad lines of an agreement had indeed been put together.

The core of the agreement was predicated on the model established by the Camp David Accords in 1978. Palestinian self-rule was to be established in the West Bank and the Gaza Strip for a transitional period of five years. At the end of the second year, negotiations would begin over final-status issues. Israeli military forces would be redeployed in several stages—from Gaza, then from Palestinian cities in the West Bank, and then in a series of "further redeployments" during the final-status negotiations. Israeli settlements on the West Bank would not be affected, and their future, as well as the issues of Jerusalem, of water rights, and of refugees, would be addressed in the final-status negotiations.

But the agreement taking shape in Oslo was different from the autonomy plan of 1978–79 in several significant respects. For one thing, the PLO had earlier refused to endorse the autonomy agreement, and Israel was led by a government resigned to the need to prevent Palestinian statehood. But the Oslo Accords were signed by the PLO and by Israeli leaders determined to effect a historic compromise with Palestinian nationalism and aware that an agreement on self-rule would likely lead to Palestinian statehood.

It was precisely his realization of the magnitude of the issues involved in the Oslo Accords that led Rabin to resort to an unusual measure: before an agreement was concluded in Oslo, he wanted to establish whether Israel had any option vis-à-vis Syria. On August 3, during a meeting in his office in Jerusalem with Warren Christopher, he asked the secretary of state to use the "hypothetical-question" technique when he went next to Damascus. As we have seen, the effort during the previous few months to develop an effective Israeli-Syrian communication had been made to no avail. Rabin now asked Secretary Christopher to inquire of Assad whether, "on the assumption that his own demand would be met," he would be willing to make peace with Israel on the basis of terms acceptable to Israel.

Rabin modeled the terms on the Israeli-Egyptian peace treaty of 1979—contractual peace, full diplomatic relations, normalization, security arrangements, implementation in phases over a five-year period, and "interface"—a heavy dose of normalization at the outset in return for a very small withdrawal on Israel's part, to enable Israel to "test" the new relationship before withdrawing from the rest of the territory it had seized in the war. Rabin emphasized to Christopher that this must remain secret, that it was a hypothetical question, and that, since he had not presented it as part of his platform in the 1992 elections, he would have to submit such an agreement to a referendum before it had legitimacy.

Secretary Christopher and Dennis Ross presented Rabin's hypothetical gambit to Assad on August 4 and returned to Rabin's office on August 5 with a response that they regarded as positive and he viewed as disappointing. Assad envisaged an implementation period of six months rather than five years; he took exception to the term "normalization"; security arrangements were welcome as long as they were for both parties and "on equal footing"; and the notion of "interface" was unacceptable. Assad clearly thought he was beginning a protracted bargaining process, but this was totally unacceptable to Rabin. Not only did he not want a lengthy and arduous tug-of-war over every issue, big or small, but he felt it was an inherently flawed process. Since Syria regarded full Israeli withdrawal from the Golan Heights as a given, the bargaining process would be restricted solely to Israel's terms, which were bound to be whittled down. Christopher and Ross went back home and left on their summer vacations—only to find out later in August that Israel had gone ahead and concluded the Oslo Accords.[10]

Still, the Clinton administration had been briefed in general terms about the secret negotiations between Israel and the PLO. In fact, Rabin and Christopher had discussed them on August 3, but the briefings were vague enough so that the Oslo breakthrough was a surprise. But the administration wasted no time in being surprised, disappointed, or angry: most of its decision-makers and policy-makers had thought a Syrian-Israeli agreement was the best starting point, but they recognized the historic significance and policy implications of Israel's agreement with the PLO. After the Israeli and Norwegian ministers of foreign affairs briefed Christopher and Ross in California, the administration decided not only to endorse the Oslo Accords but to endow them with the added value of an impressive signing ceremony on the White House lawn on September 13.

From that point on, the Israeli-Arab peace process was predicated on the Israeli-Palestinian agreement, and prospects for an Israeli-Syrian agreement diminished. Hafez al-Assad's positions and attitudes, as revealed by the hypothetical exercise in August, had had a chilling effect on Rabin, who also felt that he could not "overload the circuits" in Israel itself, that the Palestinian settlement had to be digested before a second painful concession could be accepted in Israel.

But Assad and the Clinton administration had a different idea. Assad chose to ignore the distinction between a hypothetical deposition with an honest broker and an actual commitment made in the course of a negotiation. His position was reinforced by Christopher's view—a promising start unnecessarily nipped in the bud—and his determination to go ahead with Israeli-Syrian talks once the Oslo Accords were signed. The Americans invested considerable efforts in placating Assad, persuading him not to agitate against Oslo and in fact to send his ambassador in

Washington to the signing ceremony. They also promised Assad to resume the work begun in August, and indeed they obtained Rabin's commitment to cooperate in new talks in four months. This is how the term "commitment" was introduced into the vocabulary of the Israeli-Syrian negotiation.

Fourteen months after taking office, Rabin thus effected the first breakthrough toward peace. The Oslo Accords and the Washington signing ceremony were momentous: the ground had been laid for a historic compromise between Israeli and Palestinian nationalism; by addressing this core issue and by going through the rites of mutual recognition with the PLO, Israel also laid the groundwork for normalizing its relations with other Arab states and its own international position, while Palestinians for the first time since 1947 had a real chance for statehood.

The prospects were exhilarating, but the euphoria of the moment could not conceal the gravity of the remaining problems or the difficulties inherent in the very wording of the Oslo Accords. Compromises and concessions generated criticism on both sides; criticism and opposition were bound to increase after the initial shock wore off and problems of implementation came to the fore. There was an ironic symmetry to the criticism leveled at Rabin by his Israeli critics and at Arafat by his Arab ones: Rabin was accused of making an agreement with the leader and organization he himself had demonized, endowing them with legitimacy, giving away parts of the Jews' historic homeland, and undermining the security of Israel and Israelis. Arafat was charged with having sold out, offering Israel legitimacy and recognition in return for self-rule under Israeli tutelage, abandoning the Palestinian diaspora, and relegating Palestine's crucial final status to an ill-defined future moment.

Now the principles in the Oslo Accords would have to be converted into detailed, agreed-on implementations. This required a sense of partnership and genuine cooperation. In the absence of clarity about the future, both leaders would have to win each other's confidence while keeping the support of their own constituencies. Yet, throughout the West Bank and the Gaza Strip, Israeli settlers and Palestinian Arabs would pursue different, often contradictory agendas. The PLO's former foot soldiers were to become a gendarmerie entrusted with keeping law and order but also with foiling attacks against Israel and Israelis. Important questions would have to be answered by both parties. Would Arafat actually move to Gaza and turn the Palestinian Authority there into the center of Palestinian life, or would he keep the PLO headquarters in Tunis and its "embassies" and offices around the world as the real locus of Palestinian nationalism? Would the Israeli public re-elect the government that had signed the Oslo Accords, or would the critics come to power to stop the process before the final-status negotiations?

THE CRUCIAL YEAR OF 1994

Some of these questions were answered during the following year, which Israel and the PLO spent negotiating the implementation agreement for a Gaza and Jericho plan (it was signed on May 4, 1994, in Cairo), and the Paris Agreement, which regulated economic relations between Israel and the Palestinian Authority. This was arduous work, and yet the first phase was concluded successfully: by the summer of 1994, there was a functioning Palestinian administration in Gaza and a less significant extension in Jericho. Arafat had moved to Gaza and was spending most of his time there.

But some of the anticipated difficulties arose as well. Chief among them were violent efforts made to derail the peace process. On February 25, a Jewish settler killed twenty-nine Muslim worshippers at the Tomb of the Patriarchs in Hebron; a few weeks later, on April 6 and 13, Hamas killed twelve Israelis in suicide bombings in two Israeli towns.

Israel's next major initiative was to seek a full-fledged peace settlement with Jordan, a popular, noncontroversial move that would require only moderate concessions in return for which Israel would have peace along its longest border, the prospect of warm relations and actual cooperation with King Hussein's friendly regime, and increased leverage with both Syria and the Palestinians.[11] But several significant obstacles had to be overcome first. One was the Clinton administration's reservations. It felt beholden to Syria: it wanted to hold Rabin to his commitment first to resume serious give-and-take with Assad once the agreement with the PLO was in place. It also doubted that Jordan would make a full peace; after all, the Hashemite kings had not yet done so despite decades of secret diplomacy. Also, there were disputes over land and water that had to be resolved, and to help in this Jordan would have to defy Syria and move on its own.

But Rabin persisted. He saw the advantage in several developments. King Hussein was not pleased with the Oslo Accords and the prospect it gave of a Palestinian state on Jordan's border claiming the allegiance of most of his subjects. But once his government overcame its initial anger, the members understood the advantages of having a close working relationship with Rabin during this crucial period, and the Americans, despite their reservations and different priorities, were finally persuaded to offer support: Jordan was offered debt relief, the possibility of strengthening and modernizing its armed forces, and, not least, an opportunity to erase the negative legacy of its role in the Gulf crisis and during the Gulf War period. Israel had experienced a long tradition of secret personal diplomacy with Jordan. So the talks in Washington were sidestepped during 1994 by personal diplomacy at the highest level, which achieved the breakthrough; the official delegations resumed work in earnest only at the final phases, and not in Washington. And the warm personal relationship between King Hussein and Prime Minister Rabin was indispensable in the two countries' completion of a peace treaty in one year; it was signed in October 1994.

The character and pace of Israel's negotiations with Syria were very different. In late April, when the Cairo Agreement with the Palestinians was about to be signed, Rabin was stunned to hear from Secretary Christopher that Assad had a new precondition for resumed negotiations: the full withdrawal, conditionally and hypothetically suggested by Israel via the United States in August 1993, must mean withdrawal to the lines of June 4, 1967, that is, *before* the 1967 war. The difficult truth was that between Israel and Syria there was no established border.

A line separating Mandate Syria from Mandate Palestine
had been drawn in 1923; the 1948 war had ended with an
armistice agreement, in 1949, that in certain respects was
ambiguous: it referred specifically to an "armistice line,"
leaving the border issue for future settlements. Then, between 1949 and 1967, Syria took advantage of superior
topographical conditions to establish itself in the al-
Hamma enclave in the southern foothills of the Golan
Heights and on the eastern shore of Lake Tiberias, Israel's
most important water reservoir. The term "lines of June 4,
1967," which presumed this territory was Syrian, had appeared before in the Israel-Syria negotiations, but the cut-
ting edge of Syria's demand had all along been "full
withdrawal." Syria's insistence now on the June 4 lines
could be explained as tactical (a desire to do better than
Egypt, which had made its peace according to the international border) or principled (in line with Assad's traditional
railing against the region's partition by the colonial powers). But in any event Rabin viewed it as unjustified and
illegitimate; to him it cast doubts on Assad's intention
actually to conclude an agreement, let alone swiftly, and it
reinforced his sense that an Israel-Syria agreement was
not likely during his first term.

Still, Rabin was not interested in pushing Assad into a
corner or in straining his relationship with the Clinton administration, which, from its remote and lofty vantage
point, saw little difference between the acknowledged international border and the June 4 lines. By July 19, a formula had been found for grafting the lines of June 4 onto
the original hypothetical, conditional suggestion made in
August 1993. Assad now authorized his ambassador in
Washington, Walid Muallem, to open an "ambassadors'

channel" with his Israeli counterpart, the present author. We met regularly and frequently for several months, always in the presence of one or two American diplomats. This ambassadors' channel proved to be most effective: the two nations could with relative ease explore each other's real positions and establish the possibilities and limitations of any future relationship.

CASABLANCA AND AFTER

On October 31, 1994, shortly after Jordan and Israel signed a peace agreement, the first Middle East Economic Conference opened in Casablanca. Several themes converged here: one was the notion of "Arab-Israeli normalization," which Israel's agreement with the PLO had made much easier to implement; another was the idea of having multilateral talks in which Israel, various Arab countries, and other nations discussed regional issues and means of cooperation which among other things would facilitate any concessions made in bilateral negotiations. A third idea, identified closely with Foreign Minister Peres, was that a durable Arab-Israeli peace should rest on a common effort to resolve regional socioeconomic problems and to elevate the general population's standard of living. A calmer and better integrated Middle East was a positive idea for everyone.

In many respects, the Jordan-Israel peace and the Casablanca Conference were the high-water marks of the 1992–96 period. Soon several negative trends became apparent, and two of them were devastating. But first there was the signing on September 28, 1995, of Oslo II—the agreement that extended Palestinian self-rule to the West Bank. The negotiations had been more difficult and more protracted than expected. The implementation of the Cairo Agreement had been considered fairly successful, and a sense of partnership did develop at least among some of the Israeli and Palestinian decision-makers and negotiators, but several obstacles obstructed the next phase. To begin with, the implementation of Palestinian self-rule in the West Bank was a more complex and difficult matter than in Gaza, which is a more compact area where the number of Israeli settlements and settlers is smaller. The West Bank is close to Israel's main cities, contiguous to Jerusalem, and dotted with Israeli settlements large and small. The Palestinian negotiators were eager to control as much territory as possible before the final-status talks began and before the Israeli elections, both scheduled for 1996. Rabin and Peres were equally determined to keep as many bargaining assets as they could for as long as possible.

The core of the agreement finally reached stipulated a division of the West Bank into several categories: Area A would consist of the main cities, in which a full transfer of civil and security authority to the Palestinian Authority (PA) would take place gradually as Israel withdrew; Area B would include more than 450 villages under the PA's civil authority, but with Israel maintaining overall responsibility for security until mid-1997; Area C would include state lands, thinly populated areas, and the Jewish settlements, which would remain under full Israeli security jurisdiction, with a limited PA jurisdiction over the area's sparse Palestinian population. All told, less than 30 percent of the West Bank would be transferred to direct Palestinian control at that phase.

Later on, Israel was to continue its withdrawal in three further redeployments. Israeli negotiators agreed to this scheme, which the Palestinians argued was predicated on the autonomy plan in the 1978 Camp David Accords ("a withdrawal of Israeli armed forces will take place and there will be a redeployment of the remaining Israeli forces into specified security locations"), but only at a later date and in circumstances that have since become controversial in Israel. The logic underlying Israel's acceptance of the arrangement was intimately linked to its anticipation of the final-status negotiations: every Israeli withdrawal should facilitate a concession that Arafat would have to make if those negotiations were to succeed. Another important stipulation of the agreement concerned the election, under international supervision, of an eighty-two-member legislative council, to be held twenty-two days after Israeli soldiers had withdrawn from the main cities of the West Bank (except Hebron).

This Oslo II agreement was a particularly important milestone. The original Oslo Accords had had far-reaching *potential* consequences, but actually getting through the first phase of implementation to the second was not inevitable; the second agreement provided for that transition and brought the Palestinians to the verge of statehood. Israeli negotiators defined it as "a historical agreement that put an end to the Israeli domination of the Palestinians and to the concept of the 'Land of Israel' and which set in motion the beginning of cooperation between the two peoples who decided to divide the land between them for the sake of the mutual object of peace, security and economic development."[12]

The next phase of negotiations coincided with the temporary collapse of those between Israel and Syria. Between November 1994 and June 1995, significant efforts were made to develop a dialogue between the security establishments of the two countries: the relatively open discussion between the ambassadors in Washington had clearly demonstrated that this was indispensable to any real progress. So, in December 1994, a first meeting was held between the chiefs of staff of Israel and Syria. This important and "normal" act revealed the depth of the gap separating the two protagonists' view of the security issue. Syria insisted on full Israeli withdrawal from the Golan Heights, of course, but maintained that this did not require extensive security arrangements, which would be invasive and humiliating given that Israel enjoyed overall military superiority. For Israelis who viewed the Golan Heights primarily as a security necessity, withdrawal from most, let alone all, of it would obviously have to be offset by an impressive array of other security arrangements.

President Assad, unhappy with what he regarded as excessive Israeli expectations and demands, suspended further negotiations between the military officers and insisted that a set of underlying principles be agreed upon before they met again. Most of the principles important to Assad were quite acceptable to Israel, as it happened, but for more than four months Assad's insistence that Israel agree to so-called equality as an underlying principle proved to be an insurmountable obstacle: Rabin held that, though most security arrangements could be imple-

mented on an equal basis, their *territorial* dimensions
could not be equal, because of the two countries' differences in size and topography. In May 1995, a compromise
formula was finally worked out, which led to the drafting
of a "nonpaper" on "the aims and principles of the security
arrangements."

After this, the Syrian and Israeli chiefs of staff met
again—in Washington in June. A genuine give-and-take
developed in the course of that meeting, but afterward
misunderstanding and disagreement recurred. Assad now
wanted Israel to give up its own demand for a manned
early-warning station on the Golan Heights before any
further discussions ensued. Rabin refused to comply with
this negotiating style and insisted that the sequence
agreed on in May be kept. On this sticking point the negotiation was stalled, and it was renewed only after Rabin's
assassination.

By that time, several other negative developments had
occurred. Foremost among them was a string of terrorist
attacks launched by Hamas. In October 1994, twenty-two
Israelis were killed by a suicide attack on a bus at the very
center of Tel Aviv; in January 1995, twenty-one Israeli soldiers were killed when two explosive charges were deto-
nated in a bus station; and in July, five Israelis were killed
in another suicide bombing in a bus in the city of Ramat
Gan, near Tel Aviv.

These terrorist attacks had a devastating effect on the
Israeli public's attitude toward the unfolding possibility of
peace with the Arabs. Not all of the attacks originated in
areas under the Palestinian Authority's control, but the
prevailing perception was that they did, that Arafat and his
colleagues were not totally committed to preventing anti-

Israeli terrorism by Muslim fundamentalist opponents of
the peace process, that Arafat did not consider Hamas a
dangerous challenge whose infrastructure and ideology
had to be uprooted lest his own strategy be destroyed, but
as a legitimate, significant political force he would rather
co-opt than fight head-on, as a potential partner if his
agreement with Israel collapsed.

Arafat's familiar proclivity to equivocate in difficult and
complex situations was, indeed, compounded by issues
that grew out of the Oslo Accords, though not exactly as
the Israeli public perceived it. Oslo, being a phased conditional formula for resolving the Israeli-Palestinian conflict,
required Arafat to deal simultaneously with two conflicting constituencies. He had to persuade Israel that he had
buried the hatchet and was a partner solicitous of Israeli
security, but he also felt that he had to keep the Palestinians mobilized and motivated for the tug-of-war with Israel
that lay ahead. Whatever his sense of partnership with the
Rabin-Peres government, Arafat knew well that profound
disagreements could be expected over the final-status issues. Meanwhile, his promises and exhortations to his
Palestinian constituency—the struggle continues, it's a *jihad* (holy war), we know from Islamic history that agreements made with infidels may not be binding, Jerusalem
will be liberated—were noted and amplified by Israeli opponents of the very idea of making peace with Arabs.

This was embarrassing to the Israeli government, but
not as devastating as was the reformulation of the security
issue, which occurred as an unanticipated consequence of
the Oslo Accords. Rabin, a leader preoccupied with national security, oversaw the government's effort to guarantee that reconciliation with Palestinians would have no

adverse effects on Israel's national security. He also believed that peace with the Palestinians and Israel's other immediate neighbors would set the stage for dealing with the more serious, even existential threats presented by Iraq and Iran. But he failed to foresee that a terrorist campaign in Israel proper might be launched by Arab and Muslim enemies of the peace process, and Israel had no answer to the suicide bombings. During the six years of the *intifada*, 172 Israelis were killed; in 1993–96, close to 300 Israelis were killed by terrorists. As a result, many Israelis began to equate the Oslo peace process with an actual loss of personal security. Whatever the immediate or more remote benefits accruing to Israel and to themselves from the Oslo Accords, they were less palpable and seemed less significant than this, not to mention the apparent new dependence on the Palestinian Authority's cooperation for security, not only in the West Bank but in general.

By the summer of 1995, public disenchantment with the implementation of the Oslo Accords and growing opposition to the idea of withdrawal from the Golan Heights began to erode the government's support base and legitimacy. The Oslo II agreement was only barely approved in the Knesset, and the government was only barely able to fend off an attempt by the "Golan Lobby" to entrench the 1981 Golan Law, which extended Israeli law to the Golan Heights. This would have been a mortal blow to the beleaguered Israeli-Syrian negotiation.

More ominously, opposition to the government's peace policies was becoming still uglier and more vehement. There were violent demonstrations, calls for civil disobedience (a concept imported from the United States), disruption of public order, and much incendiary rhetoric. As it turned out, in this context of violence, delegitimization, and demonization a small fanatical group was operating with the belief that the only way to stop the peace process was to assassinate Yitzhak Rabin. One of its members acted on November 4, and his action proved, indeed, to be terribly effective.

The declining fortunes of the peace process in Israel were matched by growing opposition and eroding support on the Arab side. Euphoria had not been part of the Arab response to the Oslo Accords from the outset, of course, and most of the Arab world wanted simply to get the conflict with Israel over with and turn its attention to other issues. It was grudgingly willing to endorse Oslo and to offer Israel a measure of acceptance and normalization, but even this grudging acceptance was never universal. Soon it was clouded still further by criticism of the Oslo Accords themselves, by Syria's unhappiness with the failure to achieve progress, by Islamic and other radical agitation, and by both popular and official fear that normalization might lead to Israel's domination of the Middle East. Israel's massive participation at the Casablanca Conference and some less-than-tactful rhetoric in Israel fanned these anxieties. The term "New Middle East," used by Shimon Peres as the title of a book outlining his vision of peace in the region, became the focus of this criticism of Israel's intentions.[13] Peres had wanted to propose a future in which Israelis and Arabs worked together to resolve the region's underlying problems, first and foremost poverty and scarcity of natural resources, but his book and the ideas it expounded were received by a suspicious Arab world as paternalistic at best or, more commonly and at worst, as demonstrating Israel's quest for hegemony. As Hafez al-Assad put it in an interview in *Al-Ahram*:

> I believe that they want a dark future for us. . . . I believe that the long-term goal of the others is to cancel what is called the Arabs, what is called Arabism. . . . I mean canceling our feelings as a nation, canceling Arab feelings, canceling pan-Arab identity. . . .
>
> We, as Arabs, certainly reject this because . . . Arabism is not a commodity to trade in even though this is what the others seek.[14]

Egypt played a significant part in the development of this attitude. During the previous fifteen years, Egypt had been embarrassed by its separate peace with Israel and criticized Israel for failing to implement the Palestinian part of it. Now, with a larger peace process unfolding, and when an Israeli-Palestinian agreement had been signed, with Egypt's help and support, the nation was visibly unhappy with the restructuring of regional politics, and Cairo, too, saw Israel as striving for regional hegemony at its expense. It did nothing to improve its own bilateral relationship with Israel, and waged a vociferous campaign against Israel's potential as a nuclear power, noting its policy of studied ambiguity about nuclear weapons and its refusal to sign the Treaty on Non-Proliferation of Nuclear Weapons. Egypt tried to obstruct Washington's policy of extending the terms of that treaty indefinitely upon the expiration in 1995 of its original time frame and, when this failed, suspended its participation in the multilateral working group on arms control and regional security. In the event, this Egyptian policy resulted in the suspension of all the multilateral tracks on which Israeli-Arab negotiations had been proceeding.[15]

Rabin's assassination thus happened when the peace process he had launched was already receding, and dealt it a near-fatal blow. Peres's attempt to revitalize and accelerate peace negotiations can be viewed in retrospect as its Indian summer.

AFTER RABIN

Throughout all this period and for everyone involved, domestic politics and foreign policy were closely intertwined. This was especially true between Rabin's assassination and the Israeli elections. Shimon Peres, as Rabin's successor, had to make an early dual decision: when the next Israeli election should be held and on what platform he would run. If he called an early election, he would run as Rabin's avenger and the principal issues would be the government's support of the Oslo Accords and its efforts to assign responsibility for the assassination. Or he could keep the original date—late October 1996—by which time he would have to run on his own terms and on the strength of new policy decisions he would make during the intervening months.

Peres chose the latter option, which presented him with the next decision to be made: should he seek to finalize an agreement with Syria, or should he try to speed up final-status talks with the Palestinians (scheduled to begin in

May) and seek to telescope them into the next few months?

One of Peres's closest associates, Yossi Beilin, had just concluded another secret, unauthorized negotiation with the Palestinians: he and Abu Mazen had drafted a final-status agreement, which offered the Palestinians statehood and sovereignty over most of the West Bank, though it kept most of the Jewish settlements and settlers under Israeli rule. It also proposed an ingenious solution to the issue of Jerusalem: Abu Dis, a village (or suburb) bordering Jerusalem on the east would be named Al-Quds and become a capital for the Palestinian state, contiguous to Jerusalem proper. Beilin argued that, using this draft, final-status negotiations could be completed by May, and that such an agreement would win the support of a majority of Israelis, and would give the government a program both for winning the elections in October and for consolidating the peace process.

Peres was not convinced. He preferred a different plan favored by some of his other aides and by the Clinton administration: to get a swift deal with Syria and to predicate on it a comprehensive settlement of the Arab-Israeli conflict. Peres's idea of an Israeli-Syrian settlement was quite different from what Rabin's had been. He was interested not in a lengthy phased implementation but in rapid execution, he did not see security as the key issue, and he did not believe in assigning military officers an important role in the negotiations. In keeping with his larger view, the new prime minister believed that the way to build a durable peace was to create a web of common economic interests and to increase Syria's own prosperity. There was also a significant difference in his view of "normalization." Rabin had not believed that Syria would willingly offer more normalization than Egypt had, and he thought Israel could settle, for the time being, on a formal peace. Peres held that Israel should insist on early engagement and economic cooperation, that this was the only way to deal with the underlying issues and place an ensuing settlement on a solid foundation.

Peres's preferences and his sense of urgency ran against the grain of Assad's character and style: cautious, suspicious, deliberate. Assad was attracted by Peres's apparent willingness to de-emphasize the security dimension, but he was taken aback by Peres's insistence that "normalization" and direct economic cooperation with Israel were crucial.

Just as Rabin's gambit via Secretary Christopher in August 1993 had been a breakthrough, Peres's interest in making a swift deal with Assad provided the opportunity for a second breakthrough. But prospects for an agreement soon faded. Peres explained to Secretary Christopher and his team that his willingness to come to terms with Syria was conditional on Assad's agreement to an early meeting: he knew that Assad would make peace only on the basis of Israel's full withdrawal from the Golan Heights, and he was willing to bite this bullet, but only if his own terms were met, which could be established only through negotiations; Peres wanted an early indication of seriousness, and he knew he could hardly go into the election campaign as a prime minister who had given up the Golan and gotten nothing in return.

A public meeting between himself and Assad was the litmus test. But Assad rebuffed the idea. He, too, cared

about swift negotiations and was agreeable to some relax-
ation in their format, but he would not upgrade the negotiations significantly, would not engage in serious public
diplomacy, and certainly would not meet Peres before an
agreement was reached.

Relations further deteriorated during negotiating rounds
that took place at a conference center at the Wye Plantation, near Washington (later to become much better
known), where Israel and Syria were represented by mixed
civilian and military delegations. Together with a group of
American diplomats, the two teams stayed for several days
at a time under the same roof, shared meals, and talked
more freely than they ever had before. Progress was made,
but too slowly for the Israeli government's domestic political agenda and timetable. Peres, grappling with the question of whether to move up the elections to late May,
needed to know in January whether an agreement might be
reached by the spring, so as to fit into a political schedule
leading to October elections, and the reports he received
from the Wye Plantation were not clear. Progress continued, but not much on security issues, and Syria resisted Israel's new insistence on genuine economic cooperation.

Peres therefore decided to move up the election to
May 29. This displeased Assad. (Eventually, his spokesmen would argue that an agreement had been well on its
way and that Peres's decision destroyed that prospect.)
But he agreed to continue negotiating at Wye in anticipation of the vote; negotiations continued. Israel suspended
them in early March, after the suicide bombings staged by
Hamas and Islamic Jihad in three Israeli cities in late February and early March and the Syrian delegation's refusal
to condemn them.

This terrorist wave in February and March exacted a
large number of victims, and it inflicted a deadly blow on
the peace process. Benjamin Netanyahu's victory over Shimon Peres in the May elections was the result of several
forces at work, but there can be little doubt that the suicide bombings were the single most important one. Before them, Peres enjoyed a comfortable lead (some twenty
percentage points) in the polls, but by early March that
had gone, and he never fully recovered. Netanyahu's campaign, on the other hand, used the terrorist attacks to as-
sail the credibility of Peres and his policies and to offer the
Israeli voter a magic formula of "peace with security." Netanyahu pledged to respect the Oslo Accords but to replace Peres's policy with a more aggressive insistence on
Israeli security and Palestinian compliance and a more deliberate pace in the peace negotiations. If the suicide
bombings were designed by Iran and its Palestinian clients
to stop the 1992–96 peace process, they proved to be mor-
bidly effective.

Iran's offensive against an Arab-Israeli peace was mostly
focused on Lebanon, where Hizballah had long been
Teheran's principal instrument both for expanding its influence in and through the Shi'ite community there, and
for launching attacks against Israel's "security zone" in the
south and against Israel itself. Together with the cycles of
terrorist attacks within Israel, the continuing violence
along the Israeli-Lebanese border cast an ominous
shadow on all the diplomatic maneuvers aimed at peace.
And Israelis were hard put to accept Syria's complex conduct in this matter. As the dominant power in Lebanon,
Syria could have put an end to Hizballah's attacks, but As-

sad had no intention of doing so, believing as he did in negotiating from a position of strength and in applying pressure tactics. If Israel was vulnerable to a steady stream of losses in southern Lebanon, that was all the more reason to keep the pressure on until a satisfactory agreement was reached. All the arguments made by U.S. and Israeli diplomats that this policy was undermining Assad's credibility in Israeli eyes and Israeli public support for a settlement with Syria were to no avail. Nor was Assad interested in prematurely jeopardizing his strategic alliance with Iran. If an agreement with Israel came and if a diplomatic dialogue with Washington began, a change might ensue vis-à-vis Teheran, but the prospect seemed remote.

At various points over the years, this complex Syrian policy in Lebanon became untenable. When, in late July 1993, Israel had launched a large-scale operation in southern Lebanon—Operation Accountability—Syria responded to Secretary Christopher's urging that he get Hizballah to accept "understandings" on the basis of which a cease-fire could be worked out. And from December 1995 to January 1996, at the height of its negotiation with Peres, Syria did put serious pressure and limitations on Hizballah's activities—to the point of having Iran look for alternative supply routes to its Lebanese clients, and not have things always sent by air via Damascus.

But in early 1996, yet more events—those that brought an end to the Wye Plantation negotiations—led to a further Israeli-Syrian deterioration. After the terrorist attacks in February and March, and in order to stabilize the situa-

tion and to shore up the Peres government, the Clinton
administration launched a global campaign against terrorism, inaugurated in an impressive international summit
meeting at Sharm al-Sheikh, at the tip of the Sinai Peninsula, and continued in Washington. This pushed Syria into
a dangerous corner: the campaign had a clear anti-Iran
purpose, but Assad regarded it as a hostile American-
Israeli action also aimed at isolating Syria. An emerging
strategic understanding between Israel and Turkey further
exacerbated his paranoia. He responded by giving Hizballah the green light to accelerate activity in southern
Lebanon and to launch Katyusha rockets against northern
Israel, in disregard of the "understandings" of July 1993.
In so doing, he did much to draw Prime Minister Peres to
decide on yet another large-scale operation in Lebanon—
Operation Grapes of Wrath.

Operation Grapes of Wrath is remembered primarily
for one of its tragic unintended consequences—the death
of more than a hundred Lebanese civilians by misguided
Israeli artillery shells. But it had several other significant
consequences: the alienation of Israel's Arab voters, many
of whom decided not to vote in May, and the humiliation
of Secretary Christopher by Hafez al-Assad, when the former was laboring to arrange a cease-fire and a new set of
understandings. Ironically, an improved set of understandings and a monitoring mechanism were eventually worked
out.

The monitoring agreement was drafted by diplomats
representing five countries: the United States, France, Israel, Syria, and Lebanon. It was the second text agreed
upon by Israel and Syria in a four-year negotiation that

failed to produce the agreement both countries were after. The draft was actually completed during the final days of the Peres government but was signed by Benjamin Netanyahu's government in early July. By then the Arab-Israeli peace process had shifted to a new phase.

YEARS OF STAGNATION

On October 24, 1998, a memorandum was signed in the East Wing of the White House after nine days of tripartite American-Israeli-Palestinian negotiations at the Wye Plantation conference center. At the core of it was an Israeli agreement to transfer control within three months of 13 percent of the West Bank to the Palestinian Authority. In return, the latter agreed to wage a genuine campaign against the fundamentalist Islamic and terrorist opponents of the peace process, once again to make a ceremonious revocation of the offensive paragraphs of the Palestinian National Charter that called for the elimination of the Israeli state, and, apparently, also to abstain from proclaiming statehood on May 4, 1999, which was the end of the five-year transitional period stipulated at Oslo. This agreement ended nearly two years of stalemate during which the very future of the Oslo Accords and of peace in the Middle East was in question. It brought Israeli-Palestinian relations back to the track charted by the Oslo Accords and, in so doing, set the stage for final-status negotiations; it postponed, though it did not eliminate, the dangers of a crisis over the unknown circumstances of May 1999.[1]

It was significant that it was a right-wing Israeli prime minister who grudgingly handed over the city of Hebron to the Palestinian Authority, committed his country in January 1997 to further implementation of the Oslo Accords, and then in October 1998 signed a broader agreement in which he once again committed himself to the "Oslo process," now modified to meet his demands and requirements. Yet Benjamin Netanyahu's words and actions after signing the Wye Agreement did not reflect a conversion to a belief in a genuine political settlement with the Palestinians or a sense that Yasser Arafat was and should be his partner in this process. It was difficult to know whether his rhetoric after signing the memorandum was triggering a lingering resistance in an ideological leader who had journeyed from the right wing to the pragmatic center, or was a political tactic designed to keep his reluctant Cabinet and uneasy coalition together.

By the same token, it was difficult to know how authentic was Yasser Arafat's commitment to dealing with the Palestinian foes of the peace process and to ending the ambiguity and ambivalence that he himself had exuded about reconciliation with Israel. It was important for Arafat to rally his own constituents and not to appear as an Israeli accomplice and collaborator. But did he decide to establish a single line of authority, to confront the fundamentalist opposition, and to reach out to the Israeli public, or was he merely offering temporary concessions to a right-wing Israeli leader in order to get an additional

13 percent of the West Bank on the road to statehood and independence?

It is easier to understand and explain Arafat's acceptance of the terms of the Wye Agreement than to trace the path that led his Israeli counterpart to it, after total opposition to the Oslo Accords and to any territorial concessions in the West Bank. Three years after coming to power, Benjamin Netanyahu remains an enigmatic figure, the object of bitter controversies, a prime minister who leads his country through a complex and crucial period without a clear and credible articulation of his goal.

A great deal happened in the Middle East, and in Arab-Israeli relations, in the years after May 1996—with the electoral defeat of Shimon Peres and the peace policies he represented, the Arab world's complex reaction to Netanyahu's victory, and the transition from the first to the second Clinton administration and to a different U.S. policy about the peace process. But the dominant developments are two interrelated ones: the deliberate slowdown of the peace process, which brought it to the verge of collapse; and the effective, albeit reluctant endorsement of the "Oslo process" by part of the Israeli right wing. Netanyahu is central to both developments.[2]

Netanyahu came to power at the age of forty-six, Israel's youngest prime minister. His victory in the elections of May 29, 1996, was the culmination of a stunning thirteen-year drive for political power. In 1983, Netanyahu was drafted by Moshe Arens, then Israel's ambassador to the United States and a future defense and foreign minister in Likud governments. Arens was making a systematic effort to bring back to the fold the offspring of former Revisionist Movement or Herut Party leaders who had distanced themselves from Likud over the years. Netanyahu was the son of Professor Ben Zion Netanyahu, an eminent historian of medieval Spanish Jewry and a prominent disciple of Ze'ev Jabotinsky, the founder of Revisionist Zionism. The elder Netanyahu, when he pronounces on Israeli politics, reveals a classic formulation of right-wing Zionism, hardly affected by the passage of time and articulated with great authority and conviction.[3] Arens brought Benjamin Netanyahu, who had lived much of his life in the United States, to the Israeli Embassy in Washington as deputy chief of mission. He subsequently served as Israel's ambassador to the United Nations, entered full-fledged politics through the Likud primaries, served as deputy foreign minister, and, in 1992, right after Likud's electoral defeat and Rabin's election, he made a successful bid for the party leadership.

In 1992–93, Netanyahu, then still leader of the opposition, wrote a book published as *A Place Among the Nations: Israel and the World,* in which he elaborated his view of Jewish history, Zionism, and the Arab-Israeli conflict and peace process. For the most part the text consists of familiar Israeli right-wing views and arguments rehearsing the case against Israel's making territorial concessions, against the notion of a Palestinian state, and for the "peace-for-peace" formula. Netanyahu was clearly assisted by researchers and professional writers, but the book reflects his personal style and formative experiences—as a politically oriented diplomat in Ronald Reagan's Washington and as an exponent of Likud views in the United Nations and at the Madrid Conference.

Genuine peace, Netanyahu argues, can be made and maintained only between democratic governments. In the absence of democracy in the Arab world, Israel cannot hope for a Western European or North American type of peace. Peace in the more modest sense of the term—absence of war—can be made and kept in the Middle East only from a position of strength and must be predicated on a bedrock of security and deterrence. The problem in the Middle East is not an Arab-Israeli territorial dispute but the Arabs' refusal to accept the reality of Israel's existence and its right to exist. But if Israel stands firm and receives full support from the West, the Arabs will come around to accept both Israel's reality and its right to exist. The West Bank and the Golan Heights are a defensive wall crucial for Israel's survival and must not be surrendered. A Palestinian state in the West Bank would present a mortal danger to Israel, and in any event there is already a Palestinian state—Jordan. The "demographic argument" made against this—that if Israel holds on to the West Bank and the Gaza Strip it will cease to be either Jewish or democratic—is a "demographic demon; a false argument."[4]

In 1993, the time of the Madrid Conference, Netanyahu's book laid out a particular strategy for Israel. The emphasis was on the Palestinian issue. The Gaza Strip was seen as the easier part: "Since administration of Gaza by its Arab residents does not pose an extraordinary security risk for Israel, it makes sense for most of the territory (with minor modifications for Jewish settlements) to be granted the fullest possible autonomy. I envision an arrangement whereby Israel would be in charge of security and foreign policy while all other areas of authority would be transferred to the self-administering authority under the rubric of Israeli sovereignty." Netanyahu further envisaged an international effort to invest in Gaza's economy, thus sparing both Gazans and Israelis the need to have Gazan workers making their daily trips to and from Israel's cities. After an interim trial period of at least ten years, "Israel could consider offering the Arabs of Gaza an even greater degree of self-rule."[5]

With regard to the far more complex problem of "the Arab residents of Judea and Samaria," Netanyahu offers a particular interpretation of the Camp David Accords. Limited autonomy for the Palestinians would give them "the ability to conduct their lives with a minimum of interference from the central government." But Israel's needs and expectations in the West Bank were far greater than in the Gaza Strip; there were security needs and the imperatives of Jewish settlement. The powers of Palestinian self-rule had to be curtailed, and freedom of movement for Israel's security forces had to be guaranteed. There could not be a contiguous area of Palestinian self-rule but "a system of four self-managing Arab counties: Jenin, Nablus, Ramallah, Hebron. . . . Together these counties encompass the great majority of the West Bank's Arab population and they take up no more than one-fifth of the land. . . . Control over vital matters would have to remain in the central Israeli government's hands."[6]

This would be an interim arrangement. Later, following twenty years of cooling off, when the final settlement is discussed, the question should be considered whether West Bank residents should be offered Israeli citizenship. Israel would justifiably insist on an oath of allegiance and on military service and full payment of taxes, and most residents of the West Bank would probably opt to retain their Jordanian citizenship.

Shortly after the publication of his book, Netanyahu was asked his response to the Oslo Accords. For several months he was hard put to cope with a dual challenge: not only had the Rabin government signed an agreement that ran against the grain of everything Netanyahu stood for and argued for, but it appeared to be riding on the crest of a major historical wave. Later, when a backlash developed in Israel and terrorist acts undermined the Israeli public's support for the Oslo Accords, Netanyahu led the opposition to the government's policies. Public-opinion polls in 1994 and 1995 showed him running neck and neck with Rabin.

Rabin's assassination in late 1995 had a devastating immediate effect on Netanyahu's standing. The Israeli public's revulsion with his political and personal affiliation with the political campaign against Rabin and with the radical right wing gave Rabin's successor an advantage, but after Peres's decision in January to advance the elections to May, a wave of terrorist attacks in three Israeli cities in late February and early March completely erased Peres's lead and placed him and Netanyahu in more or less the same position some ten weeks before the elections.

With that campaign a new electoral system was also introduced in Israel—a direct election of the prime minister. Netanyahu's victory by a very slim edge can partly be explained by the effect of the new system, by the superiority of his campaign, and by other personal, political, and social forces at work. But the May 29 elections were also a referendum on the peace process, and in that referendum the line expounded by Netanyahu won—by only sixteen thousand votes in the total electorate, but by a significant margin of some 10 percent of Jewish voters.

Netanyahu's campaign relied on mutually reinforcing positive and negative messages formulated on the basis of a shrewd reading of the average Israeli voter's frame of mind. Netanyahu continued with criticism of the Oslo Accords, yet he undertook to accept them and continue the peace process with modifications that would make it more deliberate and "secure." The Oslo Accords were binding international agreements that had been undersigned by the United States, and Netanyahu well understood that, as a serious contender for power, and certainly if elected prime minister, he could not renounce his predecessors' contractual obligations. And he also understood that, without committing himself to respect the Oslo Accords and proceed with the peace process, he could not expect to attract the floating votes at the center of the Israeli political spectrum. The slogan "secure peace" proved to be extremely effective for this crucial bloc of Israeli voters.[7]

The negative part of Netanyahu's and Likud's platform included harsh criticism not only of the Oslo Accords and the subsequent diplomatic work, but of Arafat's failure to comply with his commitments and of Peres's willingness to ignore this, of the Accords' shift of some of the responsibility for security to the Palestinian Authority, of the Israelis' ensuing loss of any sense of personal security, and of his opponents' alleged intention to "divide Jerusalem" and acquiesce in the formation of a Palestinian state. This vilification of Netanyahu's rivals and their policies proved to be very effective, as did his promise to deliver a "secure peace." But many Israelis and many of Israel's diplomatic partners wanted to know more about the candidate's specific ideas with regard to the future of the unfolding of Arab-Israeli relations. As election day drew closer, Netanyahu—in a series of interviews, in a television debate with Shimon Peres, and through the Likud Party's written platform—outlined the following strategy:

In order to resuscitate the stalled peace process, he would try, if elected prime minister, to reconvene the Madrid Conference, at which he would "suggest emphasizing several new channels through which to reduce the level of tension in the region, minimize the arms race and find ways to supervise the introduction of certain weapons. . . . This, in any event, is the right approach to dealing with Syria. An agreement based on withdrawal from the Golan in return for a peace treaty and normalization has no value. Furthermore, Syria is in fact not interested in such an arrangement. For Assad regaining the Golan is a fourth priority."[8] A normal peaceful relationship with Israel would open Syria up and endanger Assad's rule, and a peace agreement signed by a country like Syria would be no more than a piece of paper. Under these circumstances, a "nonterritorial" negotiation on issues such as security and water would suit both sides.

In a different vein, Netanyahu sought to use Washington's aversion to Syria's association with terrorist groups as both a stick and a carrot: "Just as there are no American technology transfers, oil sales or trade with Iran and Iraq, Syria should be warned that it would be subject to the same sanction." But if Syria expelled Palestinian terrorist groups from its territory and dismantled Hizballah in southern Lebanon, "there should be no reason why, after a period of time, Syria should not be removed from the State Department's terror list."

As for the Palestinians, "the Oslo Accords established facts on the ground. I am forced to accept them as starting points. A government I will lead will hold negotiations with the Palestinian Authority on a fair concept of peace. As for Arafat, it is not my heart's desire to meet him. I will meet him only if he meets all his commitments to us and if Israel's interests require that I do so."[9]

The Likud Party's issues platform expanded further on this issue: "The Government of Israel will carry out negotiations with the PA to achieve a permanent peace arrangement on condition that the Palestinians fully honor all their obligations. Most important among these are the clauses in the Palestinian Charter which call for the destruction of Israel and that they prevent terror and incitement against Israel." Israel's commitment to the Oslo Accords under a Netanyahu government was thus made contingent on the PA's compliance with its own commitments. The notion of an Israeli-Palestinian settlement was given a very narrow interpretation:

> The Government of Israel will enable the Palestinians to manage their lives freely within the framework of self-government. However, foreign affairs and defense and matters which require coordination will remain the responsibility of the State of Israel. The government will oppose the establishment of an independent Palestinian state. . . . Israel will keep its vital water resources in Judea and Samaria. . . . The IDF and other Israeli security forces will enjoy complete freedom of action . . . in all places in their strug-

gle against terror. . . . Security areas vital for the defense of Israel and Jewish settlements will remain under full Israeli sovereignty. . . . The Jordan River will be the eastern border between the State of Israel and the Hashemite Kingdom of Jordan. The Kingdom of Jordan may become a partner in the final arrangement between Israel and the Palestinians in areas agreed upon in the negotiations. . . .

. . . United and undivided Jerusalem is the capital of the State of Israel. Activities which undermine the status of Jerusalem will be banned and therefore PLO and PA institutions in the city, including the Orient House, will be closed.[10]

With regard to the policy of allowing Jews to establish settlements in the West Bank, Netanyahu was careful and evasive: "I certainly don't rule out new settlements, that's obvious. But my view about settlement activity has always been . . . that it has to be built on economic infrastructure which means larger urban centers." This settlement activity need not be a burden on the Israeli taxpayer: "One of the things I intend to do is to allow [settlement activity] through market forces. . . . I will not subordinate the government budget to it . . . but allow it simply through the release of public lands and transportation lines and allow natural growth."[11]

The positions Netanyahu presented stood in stark contrast to the policies Rabin and Peres had pursued and were clearly unacceptable to Israel's negotiating partners in the three unfinished "tracks" of the peace process—the Palestinians, Syria, and Lebanon. In the case of Syria, the substantial negotiations conducted by the Rabin and Peres governments had not produced a written agreement, and the issue was strictly one of policy: since, contrary to what Netanyahu had said, Assad was interested only in a territorial negotiation, what would both nations choose to do if Netanyahu won? Would a formula be found for resuming negotiations, would the conflict by proxy in Lebanon deteriorate into a full-blown conflict, or would the familiar mixed pattern of muted conflict and quest for negotiation continue?

The issue with the Palestinians was far more complex. Netanyahu's public positions were inconsistent with the Oslo Accords and with his promise to respect them. His commitment was couched in terms sufficiently broad to attract many Israeli voters worried that the pace of the peace process was too rapid and worried by the loss of personal security; they were willing to settle for a vague promise to negotiate for peace in a deliberate, secure way that would be acceptable to the Palestinian leadership. (Alongside his public position, Netanyahu gave private assurances to the Habad movement that he would not cede any territory in the West Bank to the Palestinians. The Habad movement was particularly active in the final phase of his campaign.) Insistence on the PA's full compliance with its contractual commitment could not be faulted—after all, agreements are signed in order to be respected— but it also provided an escape mechanism, should a new prime minister decide to suspend implementation of the Oslo Accords.

Victory only slightly moderated Netanyahu's stated positions. He realized that at least some of his convictions would have to be modified. Necessities of statecraft required him to polish some of the rough edges in the original draft of the new government's platform. But it still stated that the government would "insist on preserving [the Golan Heights] under Israeli sovereignty," though it stipulated elsewhere that "the Israeli Government will hold negotiations with Syria without any preconditions." The assertion that "the Jordan River will be Israel's eastern border" was omitted, but opposition to Palestinian statehood was retained, as was a fairly narrow concept of Palestinian self-government.[12]

But when his government's platform was published, Israel's new prime minister had in fact headed in a direction bound to lead him away from the principles and policies he had advocated prior to his election. We do not know what Netanyahu had in mind when he announced, on the eve of the elections, that despite his own opposition to the Oslo Accords he would respect them if elected. It was first and foremost a (successful) bid for centrist voters, but did Netanyahu also feel that he would in fact be fortunate to inherit a compromise with Palestinian nationalism rather than to have to make it himself, that while continuing to criticize the Oslo Accords and seeking to modify them he might actually proceed on the road to peace? Or did he perhaps toy with the idea that one could profess to accept the Oslo Accords but in effect emasculate, perhaps even destroy, the process they had set in motion?

Netanyahu's assumption of ultimate responsibility for Israel's policies in June 1996 was not a simple unilinear process. If he had not known it before, Israel's prime minister soon discovered that it was extremely difficult to get off the Oslo track. The reality of Israeli-Palestinian relations had been altered permanently—once by the *intifada* and then by the initial implementation of the Oslo Ac-

cords. To suspend further implementation was likely to
lead to conflict. Israel was infinitely stronger than the
Palestinian Authority, but could it afford the price of victory over the Palestinians? The direct cost—the effect on
Israel's relations with Jordan, Egypt, and the other Arab
powers and on Israel's international relations, particularly
vis-à-vis Washington—was prohibitively high. But there
were numerous countervailing forces—Netanyahu's personal and party legacy, the opposition of right-wing members of his Cabinet and coalition, mistakes made by the
Arab participants in the peace process.

Netanyahu took a step forward and soon thereafter
seemed to backtrack. He signed an agreement to withdraw Israeli soldiers from Hebron, and then immediately
authorized construction of a new Jewish neighborhood in
the Har Homa section of Jerusalem which was intended to
drive a wedge between the city and Arab Bethlehem. He
sent messages to Syria expressing interest in renewing negotiations, and then endorsed legislation sponsored by the
Golan Lobby intended to entrench Israel's presence on
the Golan Heights. To some extent this was political ma-
neuvering by a prime minister trying to preserve a precarious coalition, but there seemed also to be personal
vacillation. As late as August 1997, Netanyahu delivered a
speech to the graduating class of Israel's National Security
College in which he fell back on his 1993 book and argued
that peace agreements and normalization made no sense
in the Arab-Israeli context: "As long as the regimes around
us are not democratic and inherently peace-seeking we
will not be able to afford any arrangements in which the
security dimension is not dominant. No arrangement will
survive if we fail to keep security and defense zones." And

yet, fourteen months later, the very same leader signed the Wye River Memorandum and initially carried his Cabinet and coalition with him. The path that took them all from the formation of Netanyahu's government to that historic point unfolded in three phases.

EARLY TRANSITION AND ADJUSTMENT

Benjamin Netanyahu's adjustment to the reality and responsibility of power was matched by the Arab world's complex reaction to Israel's new government, then gradual adjustment to it. At first, this reaction consisted of shock and concern. Public-opinion polls had indicated since early March that Peres and Netanyahu were running neck and neck, and yet the Peres defeat came as a surprise. Arabs thought of Netanyahu as a foe of the peace process and assumed that a radical change in Israeli policies would ensue. An Arab summit conference on June 21–23 issued an explicit warning to the new Israeli government:

The Arab leaders affirm that any violation [*ikhlal*] by Israel of these principles and bases on which the peace process is founded, any retraction on the commitments, pledges, and agreements reached within the framework of this process, or any vacillation in implementing them will set back the peace process and will entail dangers and consequences that will plunge the region back into a spiral of tension and will compel all the Arab countries to reconsider the steps they have taken toward Israel within the frame-

work of the peace process. The Israeli Government
alone will be fully responsible for these consequences.[13]

But there were nuances in the various Arab reactions.
Yasser Arafat was the most anxious. He depended on Israel for implementation of the next phases of the Oslo
process, and he had come to trust Shimon Peres and his
team, with whom he presumed a final-status agreement
could be negotiated. What was he to make of Netanyahu's
criticism of the Oslo process, his opposition to Palestinian
statehood, his narrow concept of Palestinian autonomy,
and the assignments in his government given to people
and parties widely perceived as implacable opponents of
the PLO—Ariel Sharon, Rafael Eytan, and the National
Religious Party?

Egypt was more ambivalent. On the one hand, as patron of the Palestinians and needing to defend its own
peace with Israel, it feared the prospect of a deep crisis,
but there was also an element of relief. Egypt had been
visibly uncomfortable with the sweeping scope and rapid
pace of the peace process over the previous eighteen
months, and especially wary, as we have seen, of Peres's vision of "a new Middle East." President Hosni Mubarak
and his government had genuinely hoped for a Peres victory, but they could see a silver lining in his defeat: a more
modest scope and a more deliberate pace to the unfolding
developments, with Israel clearly responsible for both.

Syria was particularly strident in its criticism of the new
Israeli government. Syria had been unhappy with the two
Labor prime ministers, though both had seriously negoti-
ated with its representatives. Having refused to listen to

friendly advice about the wisdom of concluding a deal
with either of them before the elections, it now confronted an Israeli prime minister who was openly hostile
and who seemed to rule out the possibility of an Israeli-
Syrian settlement. Angry commentaries expressed Syria's
frustration, but in private its diplomats were willing to
meet with representatives of the new government in order
to divine its real intentions.

Jordan stood in a category by itself. King Hussein and
his government were the only Arab party to have supported Netanyahu during his election campaign, being
concerned that a victorious Peres would proceed swiftly to
a sweeping agreement with Syria and to the establishment
of a Palestinian state. Netanyahu managed to persuade
him that he would keep the peace process going at a level
and pace suitable to Jordan's political needs.

According to the Oslo process's agenda and schedule,
final-status talks, launched formally in May 1996, were
actually scheduled to begin in September. The interim
arrangements were supposed to end five years after the
Cairo signing of the implementation agreement, which
meant that May 4, 1999, became the target date. A major
item on the agenda was Israel's withdrawal (or redeployment, to use the vocabulary of the peace process) from
most of Hebron. Unlike the other cities of the West Bank,
Hebron, a city with about 120,000 Palestinian inhabitants,
had a Jewish settlement in its midst. The presence of this
group of radical Orthodox settlers, the city's general historic and religious significance, and the memory of the
massacre perpetrated against the city's Jewish population
in 1929 only worsened the complex issue of the Israeli
Defense Force's redeployment. Peres had not been keen

on going through with the redeployment after the election, and he passed this issue on to Netanyahu.

Upon completing the "redeployments" from the six main cities of the West Bank, the second Oslo agreement committed Israel to proceeding with three "further redeployments" prior to final-status negotiations. The origin of that idea lies in the Camp David Accords, which stipulated that during final-status negotiations Israel would withdraw its troops to "security locations"; in the summer of 1995, at a late phase of the negotiations leading to the second Oslo accord, Israel agreed to three "further redeployments," a concession that made sense only in the context of a genuine final-status negotiation: if Israel were to hand over most of the West Bank to Palestinian Authority control, it might as well do it in phases, and use the phasing as a way of facilitating the concessions Arafat would have to make, too. But for a government formally opposed to Palestinian statehood and committed to a narrow view of Palestinian self-government, this notion made little or no sense.

Netanyahu was, indeed, determined to change both the agenda and the pace of Israeli-Palestinian diplomacy. He refused to meet with Arafat and wanted the latter to settle for lesser officials—first his own policy adviser (June 28), then the foreign and defense ministers (July 23 and September 18, respectively). He indicated several times that he was in no hurry about redeployment in Hebron, a complex issue. Most significantly, he insisted on "reciprocity" and "compliance," themes that had figured prominently in his election campaign, when he had accused Peres of being too lenient and of being willing to overlook Arafat's and the PA's failure to discipline or control terrorist organizations that struck at Israel, failure to complete the revision of the Palestinian National Charter, and failure to cease its hostile propaganda against Israel. He now demanded that the Palestinians comply "fully" with these commitments before Israel took another step.

A demand for full compliance with an agreement is, of course, perfectly valid. But, given the context in which the demand was made, Palestinians, Arabs in general, and the world at large saw this as an attempt to change the rules of the Israeli-Palestinian game. Rabin and Peres had argued that Israel, as the senior and more powerful party to the agreement, did not have to insist on a literal interpretation and implementation. The shift from that approach to a strict insistence on "full compliance" was widely perceived as a manifestation of the new government's negative attitude and of its proclivity to use Israel's preponderance vis-à-vis the Palestinians to impose rather than negotiate a settlement.

The awkwardness of Israel's relationship with the Palestinians was matched by dim prospects with Syria. The new prime minister was now fully briefed on the course of the 1993–96 negotiation. He knew that Hafez al-Assad was willing to make peace with Israel but only on the basis of the latter's complete withdrawal from the Golan Heights. Assad now demanded also that the new government endorse the whole legacy of the negotiation conducted by its predecessor and commit itself to that full withdrawal. Netanyahu knew very well that the positions he himself had advocated with regard to Syria and the Golan Heights were not realistic, but he was not willing to accept this de-

mand. Assad, grasping the full significance of the change
in Israel, rather than modify his position chose to dig in
more firmly.[14]

In late July, Netanyahu tried a different approach. An
agreement would be worked out that would have Israel
withdraw its soldiers from the "security zone" in southern
Lebanon: this would be conceived and perceived as a first,
"confidence-building" phase in a broader Israeli-Syrian
settlement (hence the name "Lebanon First" given to this
initiative). The idea was stillborn. In fact, it was not a new
idea, and Syria had systematically obstructed earlier attempts to break the logjam in this fashion. As Syria saw it,
Israel's predicament in Lebanon was Syria's most effective
instrument for pressuring Israel to move in the Golan
Heights, and it was not about to give this up. Furthermore, it suspected that a separate Israeli-Lebanese negotiation would be used to lure Lebanon away from Syria. It
lost no time in foiling the new Israeli initiative.

Nor was Netanyahu successful in building his relations
with Jordan's King Hussein and Egypt's President Mubarak. With the passage of time, and as Netanyahu's
Palestinian policy became more evident, Cairo and Amman expressed disappointment and criticism; both could
live with a virtual suspension of Israeli-Syrian negotiations, but neither could accept Israel's new policy toward
the Palestinians. Egypt's anger was contained—Cairo had
a stake in Arafat's success but was content to take advantage of the new turn of events in order to slow down "normalization" of Israel's position in the region. For Jordan, the
political challenge was much more acute. Given that
the majority of Jordan's citizenry was Palestinian and given
the criticism the king had endured for making a peace

with Israel, he believed that a suspension or collapse of Israeli-Palestinian efforts could undermine his own position. He expected subtlety from Netanyahu; he had wanted more deliberation and modesty in Israeli diplomacy, and he had not expected such a dramatic reversal of policy.[15]

This transitional phase was terminated in September by two unrelated developments, the first between Israel and Syria, which brought the two countries to the verge of military confrontation.

This was a classic case of an unintended escalation nourished by misperceptions and mutual suspicions—all this exacerbated by the new Israeli leaders' inexperience and the Syrian leaders' unfamiliarity with their counterparts. A redeployment of Syrian troops from Beirut to the Beqaa Valley in eastern Lebanon, close to the Syrian border, had been planned for some time as a demonstration of the incremental normalization of life in Lebanon. But on the other side of the border, it was seen as a potential buildup for a surprise attack against Israel. In turn, Syrians, knowing there were no offensive intentions on Syria's part, saw Israel's deployment for such an eventuality as preparation for a potential attack. This spiral of mutual suspicion threatened to escalate into real hostilities. The tension eventually eased, but the episode demonstrated the dangerous potential in the Israeli-Syrian relationship, particularly when there was no ongoing direct dialogue between the two.

The other development was much graver. On September 24, the Israeli authorities opened for public viewing and in the service of tourism the Hasmonean Tunnel, which runs from the Western Wall along the base of Temple Mount. The tunnel, of immense archeological interest,

had been readied for opening during Rabin's tenure, but
government policy then had been not to open the tunnel
except in coordination with the Palestinian Authority.
Given Arab, Muslim, and international sensibilities regarding anything that had to do with the holy places in
Jerusalem, it was decided to wait for the right moment;
the tunnel and its opening would not in any case interfere
with the status quo in Jerusalem. The Netanyahu government's decision to disregard these considerations to open
the tunnel on September 24 as an assertion of Israel's sovereignty in Jerusalem was yet another symptom of its inexperience, and it played directly into Arafat's hands. Arafat
saw a golden opportunity to reverse the rules of the game
that Netanyahu had played since June. He called for
protest marches denouncing the tunnel opening as a "big
crime against our religion and our holy places." In the following five days of violence, fifteen Israeli soldiers and
sixty Palestinians were killed. Some of the violence was
spontaneous, but there is little doubt that the Palestinian
security officers who took an active part in the fighting
were in most cases authorized if not encouraged to do so
by Arafat.

By reacting in this fashion, Arafat may well have damaged his cause in the long run. For many Israelis it was
proof that the Palestinian Authority could not be trusted
to be a genuine partner in protecting Israeli security, that
Arafat gave his cooperation only so long as his expectations were met, that if final-status negotiations were dead-
locked violence could be expected. But in the short run
his action was most effective. Netanyahu was now anxious
to talk to him. President Clinton invited both men, as well
as King Hussein and President Mubarak, to Washington

for a meeting on October 1 and 2. The Jordanian monarch accepted the invitation; Egypt's president chose not to.

THE ROAD TO THE HEBRON AGREEMENT

The Washington summit conference quickly accomplished two important goals: it defused the crisis that had erupted after the tunnel opening, and it resuscitated Israeli-Palestinian negotiations. But these were arduous, and it took three months more to reach further agreements about Israel's redeployment in Hebron and future relationship with the Palestinian Authority. Also, the Washington conference expressed important changes in Washington's outlook on and role in the Israeli-Arab peace process.

Ever since the formation of the first Clinton administration in January 1993, the Israeli-Arab peace process was high on Washington's foreign-policy agenda. The president, the secretary of state, and their assistants invested a significant portion of their time in it, and its achievements were among their most notable foreign-policy successes. Indeed, the Clinton administration's cooperation with the Rabin and Peres governments was a unique phase in American-Israeli history. In earlier stages, it invariably took American pressure on reluctant Israeli prime ministers to make territorial and other concessions in order to effect progress (even Begin's negotiation with Sadat, which had originated as an Israeli-Egyptian initiative, could not be concluded without American participation), but under Rabin and Peres the moving force was an Israeli leadership determined to move toward peace, and reconciled to the notion that both sides had to make concessions in order to reach and implement an agreement. During the Rabin years, this was buttressed by a quite warm and intimate relationship between the president and the prime minister, and the Clinton administration openly supported Peres in the 1996 election campaign.

After Netanyahu's victory, the administration felt that it had lost this secure Israeli footing. Its nervousness was exacerbated by Secretary of State Warren Christopher's disenchantment with Syria, and by changes in the Middle East (the formation of an Islamist government in Turkey, unrest in Saudi Arabia) that made it less hospitable to a major investment of U.S. efforts. As the presidential elections of November 1996 drew closer, the prospect of open disagreement with an Israeli prime minister openly allied with conservative Republicans grew more alarming. It remained important to preserve the American achievements in the Arab-Israeli peace process and to avoid its breaking down, but American willingness and ability to invest significant resources were limited.

This calculus was altered by the outburst of violence in September. Just a few weeks before the election, President Clinton took the political risk of convening a summit that could end in failure. In the event the meeting was successful, but Netanyahu's mobilization of the organized right-wing Jewish community in the United States and the Republican leadership in Congress to keep the administration at bay was a harbinger of future developments.

The Washington summit was followed by a round of intensive negotiations held at the Erez checkpoint between

Israel and Gaza. Secretary of State Christopher presided at the outset, but as the negotiations lingered on, leadership passed to the principal American negotiator, Dennis Ross. In the absence of mutual trust and effective communication between the Israeli and Palestinian leaders, the United States had to go from being a facilitator to being a combined mediator, partner, and guarantor.

One level of the negotiation dealt with the redeployment in Hebron. On another level, Arafat and the Palestinian Authority were eager to obtain control over Hebron, but they wanted also to ascertain that this would not be a final act of a moribund process, but would be fitted into a broader agreement on the implementation of Oslo II. More specifically, they demanded that a date be set for resumption of final-status negotiations, that a timetable be set for the implementation of Israel's three further redeployments, and that agreement be reached on other issues pending since 1995—the opening of air and sea ports in Gaza, the establishment of a "safe passage" between the West Bank and the Gaza Strip, and the release of Palestinian prisoners from Israeli jails.

Benjamin Netanyahu, in turn, had many dilemmas and problems. Israeli withdrawal from Hebron would be seen by many Israelis as an act of withdrawal from part of the historical, biblical Land of Israel. In agreeing to go through with the agreement to do this, he would be the first Likud leader to offer and implement such a concession. And even if he were to do so by arguing that he had no choice but to fulfill the contractual obligation undertaken by his predecessors, what was he to do about the sweeping commitment to three further redeployments?

The problem was not limited to Netanyahu's personal

soul-searching. He was the first Israeli prime minister to
have been elected by a direct popular vote, but as he and
the Israeli political system soon discovered, the new election law did not mean that the prime minister was immune to pressure from his own Cabinet and coalition;
though the law made it more difficult to unseat him than
before, he still had to form and maintain a parliamentary
coalition. Netanyahu's not very large coalition (it originally
consisted of sixty-six members) had a rightist complexion;
within it, several of his Likud colleagues and members of
the National Religious Party formed a hard core of opposition to making any territorial concessions in the West
Bank. The argument that governments are constrained by
domestic political opposition has been used all too often in
Arab-Israeli negotiations, but Netanyahu did face a genuine, significant opposition within his own party and coalition.

Netanyahu understood that he had no choice—he had
to redeploy in Hebron, and he had to reiterate the basic
Israeli commitments at Oslo II—but he fought to recast
these commitments in terms that would be or at least appear to be new and more congruent with his own outlook.
By mid-January 1997, an agreement had been reached
that was embodied in three documents: a protocol to implement the redeployment in Hebron; a "note for the
record" prepared by Dennis Ross as a summary of a meeting between Netanyahu and Arafat; and a letter from Secretary Christopher to Netanyahu. These three documents
were supplemented by two additional instruments: a letter
from Dennis Ross to the secretary of the Israeli Cabinet
that formalized the original compromise worked out by

King Hussein, suggesting that the term "mid-1998" be left
vague.

The security arrangements detailed in the protocol
were different enough from past ones to enable Netanyahu to argue that he had obtained a better, indeed satisfactory, security regime in Hebron. In the note for the
record, Israel reaffirmed its promise to proceed with implementation of Oslo II, which meant first and foremost
the three further redeployments. It undertook to carry out
the first redeployment during the first week of March, to
negotiate the other pending issues, and to resume the
permanent-status negotiations within two months of the
implementation of the Hebron protocol. Arafat, for his
part, reaffirmed the following principal promises: to complete the revision of the Palestinian National Charter, to
fight terror and prevent violence, to strengthen security
cooperation, to prevent incitement and hostile propaganda, to combat systematically and effectively terrorist
organizations and infrastructure. The note also stipulated
that "the exercise of Palestinian governmental activity
and location of Palestinian governmental offices will be
as specified in the Interim Agreement" (in the coded
language of Israeli-Palestinian relations, this meant the
Palestinian Authority's undertaking not to engage in
"governmental" activity in Jerusalem) and that Oslo II
should be implemented on the basis of "reciprocity."

That last point was repeated and reinforced in Secretary
Christopher's letter to Netanyahu. The letter was essentially intended to assuage Israelis, but it addressed a major
Palestinian concern by stating the American administration's "belief that the first phase of further redeployments

should take place as soon as possible and that all three phases of further redeployment should be completed within twelve months of the implementation of the first phase of further redeployments but no later than mid-1998." Israel, it was implied, would determine the scope of the redeployments.

The Palestinian Authority and the United States could note with satisfaction that a Likud prime minister was about to withdraw Israeli soldiers from most of Hebron and that he formally reaffirmed the principal commitments of Oslo II. Netanyahu, in turn, could claim that he had committed Arafat to respond to his criticisms of the Oslo Accords and that he had formalized the principle of reciprocity and established a formal link between Arafat's compliance with these commitments and Israel's own further undertakings. In fact, though Israel's redeployment in Hebron was carried out in accordance with the protocol, the larger agenda addressed in the note for the record and the secretary's letter was not implemented. Further progress in Israeli-Palestinian relations was delayed for nearly two years.

In other words, the Hebron Agreement ended up being only and precisely that—an agreement on Israel's redeployment in Hebron. To address and implement the larger agenda—reaffirming and implementing the unfinished components of Oslo II—the three partners to the Hebron Agreement had yet to make some fundamental decisions.

Israel's prime minister felt ill-at-ease with the agenda itself, requiring those three further redeployments by mid-1998, leaving less than a year before the end of the five-year transitional period. Israel could not realistically expect to complete the process without ceding a significant portion of the West Bank. For the first redeployment, scheduled for March 1997, Netanyahu offered 2 percent, and Arafat scornfully rebuffed this. So Netanyahu and Arafat were miles apart, and bridging the gap was likely to take a long time, and from the Israeli vantage point, giving up land in three predetermined moves made little if any sense.

Thus, in March 1997, Netanyahu proposed that Israel and the PA telescope the whole process and, instead of proceeding with the implementation of Oslo II, meet for a Camp David–style conference, allocating three to six months for completing the final-status negotiations. The underlying argument was quite persuasive. The Oslo process, it was said, had been intended to go in phases so as to build confidence between the parties; whatever its initial achievements, it was clearly not building confidence, and it ought to be replaced by something else. This valid argument was briefly endorsed by the new Secretary of State, Madeleine Albright, but it was rendered useless by one problem—mistrust. Arafat and many other Arabs had no trust in Netanyahu and his government, and they saw his offer as a transparent maneuver to extricate himself from the Oslo commitments.

This policy problem was exacerbated by a political one. Even if Netanyahu wanted to go through with genuine implementation of the Hebron accords, he might not have had a working majority in his Cabinet and coalition. One right-wing member of his party and Cabinet, Benny (Binyamin) Begin, resigned after the agreement was signed. Menachem Begin's son refused to remain a member of a government that had voted to hand over part of the Land of Israel to foreign control. Nor did Begin con-

ceal the contempt he had for Netanyahu. Other right-
wing Likud coalition members and members of the
National Religious Party threatened to topple the government if it decided on further withdrawals in the
West Bank. Their threat was aggravated by the dissension
of other Cabinet and coalition members—Finance Minister Dan Meridor resigned in June 1997 and Foreign Minister David Levy in January 1998—and others distanced
themselves due to personal differences with Netanyahu or
unhappiness with his style and performance. As time
passed, pressure built among more moderate or pragmatic
members of the government, who began to suspect that
Netanyahu had no intention of implementing the agreement. Netanyahu himself was increasingly preoccupied
with his government's survival, and his perpetual maneu-
vering created a zigzag effect: if Netanyahu signed the
Hebron Agreement in January, he tried to balance it in
February by placating his right-wing critics with the Har
Homa construction in Jerusalem. The Palestinians considered this a provocative act, and Arafat responded by
suspending the negotiations.

As might have been anticipated, the principle of reciprocity also obstructed rather than facilitated progress.
Arafat had been reluctant to take on the Islamic fundamentalist opposition to his negotiations with Israel, to
complete the revision of the Palestinian Charter, to stifle
anti-Israeli rhetoric, or to engage overtly in security cooperation with Israel. Even when things had been at their
best, he was determined to keep the option of joining
forces with the fundamentalists if things turned sour, to
keep his people mobilized, and to refrain from appearing
as an Israeli accomplice. By 1997, he must have realized

this conduct had alienated part of the Israeli public and had helped to undermine Peres and bring Netanyahu to power, but if he considered a policy change he was discouraged by his—and many others'—suspicion that Netanyahu was actually seeking to emasculate the Oslo process, in which case he was not about to alter his own conduct. And thus, throughout this period, Arafat persisted both in presuming that the Oslo process offered the best way to achieve the historic goal of Palestinian statehood, and in refusing to make any additional investment of acting on the Hebron Agreement commitments. Netanyahu argued, in turn, that, given this failure to offer "reciprocity" and "compliance," he wasn't about to have Israel make additional withdrawals.

At the core of the original Oslo process had been the idea that it took time to make a transition from conflict and hostility to a settlement predicated on compromise and partnership. These last had not always been present during the brief golden period of Israeli-Palestinian relations, but they were glaringly absent after June 1996. Any concessions made and cooperation secured were offered grudgingly. Both parties presumed they were locked in conflict, and each acted to maximize its position in the West Bank and in East Jerusalem.

Under these circumstances, it was difficult to get them to cooperate in the crucial and sensitive area of security. Given the devastating effectiveness of the Islamic terrorist campaigns of 1994–96 and the significance attached to this theme by Netanyahu, terrorist attacks were now particularly agonizing. During the first thirty months of Netanyahu's government, suicide bombings occurred in Tel Aviv and Jerusalem, though they did not have the impact

of the earlier ones—partly because of effective counter-
measures taken by Israel and at least sometimes by the
Palestinian Authority, and also through sheer luck and,
perhaps most important and ironic, the slowdown in the
peace process. Iran, Hamas, and Islamic Jihad did not
have to invest an effort comparable to that of the years
1993–96 in order to obstruct a faltering peace process.

So the security cooperation between Israel and the
Palestinian Authority was erratic. Conducted both bilater-
ally and trilaterally (with the CIA as the third party), it affected and expressed the fluctuations of the general
Israeli-Palestinian relationship. Security, after all, was at
the core of the "reciprocity" and "compliance" issues.
Arafat, in offering some cooperation some of the time,
withholding it at other times, and occasionally tolerating
or encouraging anti-Israeli violence, was walking a very
fine line. Throughout this period he continued to act on
the assumption that the Oslo process still offered the best
prospects, but favoring it was not a policy he pursued with
enthusiasm or consistency. And as time went on, his motivation changed. His primary effort became to cultivate a
new relationship with the United States and, specifically,
with the Clinton administration. The primacy of obtaining
control over additional land in the West Bank was clear,
but as long as this was not feasible, Arafat was willing to
settle, as an interim goal, on the dividends earned in a new
relationship with the world's leading power.

President Clinton had made a personal political investment in Israeli-Palestinian relations and taken some polit-

ical risks to defuse the crisis in September 1996. But if it took three months to negotiate the Hebron Agreement, only to encounter fresh difficulties and disappointments when it came to implementation, what were the prospects for the United States in the final-status negotiations?

Warren Christopher's successor, Madeleine Albright, had a different order of priorities, as was seen in her decision to delay her first trip to the Middle East (in sharp contrast to Christopher's trip to the region less than a month after the inauguration in 1993). During her first weeks in office, it became evident that only part of the Hebron Agreement would be implemented and that a fresh effort would have to be made to get the three further redeployments. This was not an attractive prospect, and it was made even less so by the Israeli government's demonstrable willingness and ability to mobilize conservative Republicans in Congress and a significant part of the organized American Jewish community against it. In theory, a president who had just been re-elected should have been immune to such considerations, but political circumstances in early 1997—and a Republican majority in both houses that enhanced the influence and importance of every single member of Congress—dissuaded the administration from open confrontation with the Israeli government. President Clinton and several of his aides made no effort to hide their criticism of Israel's prime minister and his government, though they avoided a showdown. The United States lowered its profile in the peace process but, despite criticism and advice to the contrary, refused to walk away from it. Clinton believed that the United States must make real and visible efforts to prevent the collapse of a diplomacy closely identified with the American position, and that at the end of the day Netanyahu would go through with the second redeployment.

Four factors converged in the fall of 1998 in order to bring that about.

First, Washington made it abundantly clear that, even if Arafat and the Palestinian Authority did not fully comply with their own commitments, it expected Israel to provide the key to further progress and to implement the redeployments. The American peace team established a middle ground of 13 percent as the effective range of Israel's next withdrawal in the West Bank. It brought Arafat down from his initial demand for a withdrawal from some 40 percent, it subsequently obtained Netanyahu's personal agreement to this figure, and then it set to work on constructing an agreement into which this withdrawal could be fitted and on helping Netanyahu to bring the rest of his government and coalition along.[16]

In the course of this protracted process, President Clinton was going through the first stages of his worst personal-political crisis. The Lewinsky affair exploded during Netanyahu's visit to Washington in January 1998, when the question of U.S. pressure on Israel was at the fore, and began to simmer down in the early fall of 1998, at the time of the Wye River Conference. There the president was first and foremost trying to solve a difficult and dangerous problem in the Middle East, but he was also trying to conduct normal presidential business and demonstrate his own personal effectiveness. By making the conference possible, by sustaining Clinton's personal participation, and by making their own political contributions, the president and his administration exerted an unusually effective influence on Israeli-Palestinian relations.

A second important consideration was the imminence of May 4, 1999. This date had seemed quite remote when the Hebron Agreement was completed in January 1997, but now all parties were dangerously close to the end of the transitional period. Arafat began to threaten publicly that he would announce Palestinian independence and statehood unilaterally; Israel threatened to respond with its own unilateral actions. Israel is, indeed, not short of potential responses, but a major crisis over a unilateral Palestinian declaration of independence would be undesirable for any Israeli prime minister. Arafat's and his colleagues' consternation with Israel and their own rhetoric notwithstanding, they still preferred to reach their goals by an agreement with Israel and were worried about the repercussions of a unilateral declaration. The explosive potential in this situation was fully exploited by U.S. diplomacy in bringing the parties together at the Wye Plantation.

Third, a deal was gradually crystallizing. After all, the territorial aspect of the agreement had been put together by mid-1998; it then had to be matched by a political structure that would meet Netanyahu's requirements. On the face of it, Arafat had done this when he signed the Hebron Agreement. What was the value in yet another undertaking to revise the Palestinian Charter or the practical and political value of further reaffirmations of all the old points? Yet, in substantive and political terms, it was important for Netanyahu to be able to show that Israel's territorial concession would be matched by something; on a deeper level, he and his associates had to ask themselves about the rationale of giving up 13 percent of the West

Bank at that particular juncture. Keeping a commitment,
mending relations with the United States and other nations, keeping the peace process going—these were all
weighty reasons, but they had been for years. A new
prospect was now needed for Netanyahu's government to
agree to a new situation in which the Palestinian Authority
would control 40 percent of the West Bank and have an
international airport in Gaza.

Lastly, the domestic political base in Israel for implementing the 13 percent withdrawal was put together. The
link between Netanyahu's personal and domestic political
calculus and the implementation was an especially intri-
cate business. Netanyahu had concluded earlier that what
had already been implemented as part of the Oslo process
was irreversible, and that at least part of the remaining Israeli commitments had to be implemented as well. These
conclusions were linked to a presumption that in a re-
election bid Netanyahu would need centrist as well as
right-wing votes, that he would run as a leader who had
lived up to his promises. But when would the next election
be held? Could Netanyahu keep his coalition together until 2000? Could he, more specifically, withdraw from 13
percent of the West Bank *and* keep the National Religious
Party, the settlers' movement's closest ally, in his coalition?
Or did he perhaps want an early election, right after an
agreement, in which he might lose the votes from the radical right wing but steal the Labor Party's thunder?

For many months, Netanyahu seemed to think of and
try every political option and maneuver—a "national-unity
government" with the Labor Party, splitting the Labor
Party and attracting part of its parliamentary caucus into
his coalition under the banner of "saving the peace," but-

tressing the coalition by promising its right wing to avoid, delay, or fail to implement an agreement, and promising its more pragmatic members to make the deal and carry it out. Finally, in September 1998 he decided to make Ariel Sharon, minister of national infrastructures, his main ally, and to rely on this leader of the radical right in the final stage of negotiating the agreement.

On October 14, Netanyahu appointed Sharon foreign minister; Sharon immediately announced that he would not vote for any agreement stipulating a withdrawal of more than 9 percent, but he made it clear that he would be the prime minister's partner in negotiating such an agreement at the Wye Plantation.

Sharon's own journey from right-wing radicalism to this position paralleled and supplemented Netanyahu's shift from his pre-election positions to his post-election policies. Sharon had grown up in the tradition of Labor Zionism's activist school. In 1972, having retired from the armed forces as a general, he joined Likud; he left his mark on Israel's relationship with the Arab world as the architect of the subsequent war in Lebanon and as the secular patron of the settler movement.[17]

At the age of seventy, Sharon was acting under the influence of multiple considerations. He clearly remained critical and dubious of the ongoing peace process and specifically of the two Oslo Accords. But he was also eager to rehabilitate his reputation and image that had tarnished during Israel's debacle in Lebanon in 1982–83. He also clearly relished his standing as the one substantial person in Netanyahu's government, though his relationship with Netanyahu was awkward. As a rule, he criticized him from the right, but when he had been in charge of resolving disputes between Israel and Jordan over water rights, he proved to be most accommodating.

Sharon's work in resolving the water issue and the Jordanians' exasperation with Netanyahu made Sharon a pivotal figure in Israeli-Jordanian relations. For years, this Likud leader most closely identified with the slogan "Jordan is Palestine" had been anathema to the Jordanians. But in the 1998 circumstances, they were willing to hold on to him as a pillar of effectiveness and pragmatism in the confusing landscape of Israel's new politics. As for Sharon himself, he regarded his new relationship with the Hashemites as a model for the kind of accomplishments he envisaged for himself in Israeli politics. Why couldn't he, drawing on his nationalist credentials and his gift for plain, tough talk, cast himself as the senior, mature figure of Israel's right wing who could offer the key to a reasonable compromise, a compromise for which he alone could mobilize sufficient support?

A glimpse into Sharon's recent thinking is afforded by the synopsis of a presentation distributed by his office in May 1998 under the title "Security and Coexistence: An Alternative Approach to Breaking the Deadlock Between Israel and the Palestinians." The final two paragraphs—"a summary"—read as follows:

The way I view the situation today, it is possible to reach an agreement with the Palestinians in the interim phase, which would be somewhat similar to the concept of nonbelligerency. This will give Palestinians the possibility of keeping and holding to the Oslo Accords, and Israel the necessary time to examine and see that conditions for a true and lasting peace have materialized.

Finally, I wish to emphasize that this alternative approach of crisis avoidance, and the concept of "less than peace" agreement, which I have presented here, should be considered as a *fallback position*: if at a certain point it becomes clear to all parties that the current efforts to reach an agreement fail, then I believe it would be in the interest of both Israel and the Palestinians to adopt this approach as a means of breaking the deadlock and reviving the peace process.[18]

It is apparently with this view in mind that Israel's new foreign minister went to the Wye Plantation. He is reported to have argued that any agreement reached there should be seen as an interim one for some twenty years. This is clearly not what the Palestinians, the rest of the Arab world, and the United States had in mind. Nor was it clear how Sharon and Netanyahu really viewed the agreement they concluded. Did they believe that they could freeze the status quo for so long, or did they realize that this was not the last stop in their journey toward the middle ground of pragmatism and compromise?

In stark contrast to the partial progress made in Israeli-Palestinian affairs, there was no movement whatsoever in Israel's relationship with Syria. The negotiations suspended in March 1996 were not renewed, despite several

attempts by the American peace team, the European
Union's special envoy, and a whole host of private inter-
mediaries. Technically, the chief obstacle was Syria's insistence that "the negotiations be resumed at the point at
which they had been interrupted" and Israel's rejection of
this demand and of the interpretation on which it was
based. For this terminology was coded language for a very
sweeping demand: Syria's version of the 1993–96 negotiation had it that Prime Minister Rabin had committed Israel to withdraw from the Golan Heights, that Peres had
reaffirmed this commitment, that these commitments
were legally binding, and that fresh negotiations must proceed from this point of departure. The Israeli version was
that there was no commitment, agreement, or promise to
withdraw; that a hypothetical, conditional position had
been deposited with the United States to be matched by
Syrian acceptance of a settlement package, which never
happened. Netanyahu had a letter from Secretary of State
Christopher in September 1996 expressing the view that
the only agreement reached during the negotiations, the
"nonpaper" on the security arrangements, was not legally
binding; oral exchanges were surely even less binding than
this nonpaper.

The gap between these two positions could in fact have
been bridged, but the real obstacle was not procedural but
substantive. As the negotiations of 1993–96 clearly established, President Assad was willing to sign a peace treaty
with Israel, but insisted on a full Israeli withdrawal from
the Golan Heights, and the peace package he has thus far
offered does not meet Israel's criteria. The "hypothetical
formula" facilitated negotiation, but suspension of the
talks left Syria with nothing achieved. Since June 1996,

Assad has faced an Israeli prime minister elected on a platform that explicitly precluded full withdrawal from the Golan Heights. Thus Assad now insists on an explicit (not hypothetical) American or Israeli commitment as a precondition for renewing the negotiations, but he is not anxious and certainly not desperate for this. And he is not interested in negotiations for their own sake. In his view, the very fact of holding a Syrian-Israeli negotiation would play into Netanyahu's hands, enabling him to argue that the peace process had been revived and, on that basis, to advance the cause of Arab-Israeli normalization. Assad therefore demands that a new phase of negotiations be predicated on Israel's explicit commitment to withdraw from the Golan Heights.

This has not been acceptable to Netanyahu, for two main reasons. Like his predecessors, on procedural and practical grounds he has resented Assad's attempt to dictate conditions and to open a negotiation with a guaranteed bottom line, which would leave the Israelis with very little leverage. Then there is the substantive and ultimately most important obstacle: was Netanyahu interested in and could he deliver an agreement with Syria that was predicated on Israel's withdrawal from the Golan Heights? Netanyahu had shown that he could disengage from his past record and election promises, but would he be able to make this Syrian deal? On various occasions he indicated that he was interested in a negotiation with Syria and realized that it could not be conducted effectively if he continued to hew to his past positions. He was also willing to offer various different formulations that implied an unspecified withdrawal in the Golan Heights. But he did not agree to Assad's demands.

Assad, needless to say, has been unhappy with an indefinite stalemate in which there has been some progress in Palestinian matters and none with Syria. His most effective means of putting pressure on Israel has been through Lebanon. By allowing and sometimes encouraging Hizballah to operate against Israeli forces in southern Lebanon, he has produced a steady stream of casualties, and Israel's decision-makers have to take notice. But the Israelis' sensitivity to these casualties, by now a familiar aspect of the Arab-Israeli conflict, is only worsened by the apparent senselessness of this policy. Israel's presence in the security zone of southern Lebanon had been intended not to advance a policy agenda but to maintain a status quo until conditions were ripe for a political solution, whereupon Israel would depart. Sustaining casualties for such a point is particularly onerous. Yet Israel faces only a few options here. It is broadly agreed that the only fundamental solution can be political-diplomatic, and that Syria holds the key to it. For a government and a significant portion of the public which does not wish to withdraw from the Golan Heights, however, this is not a viable possibility.

Nor is the option of escalating Israel's military responses or activities attractive to most Israelis. After Operation Litani (1978), the Lebanon war and its sequel (1982–84), Operation Accountability (1993), and Operation Grapes of Wrath (1996), the prospect of getting back or deeper into the Lebanese morass is simply not considered by most participants in the policy and public debates. A third option—having the Israeli Defense Force leave Lebanon under the aegis of an explicit or implicit understanding with the government of Lebanon—was tried in the first moments of Netanyahu's government and was rebuffed by

Syria. A second effort was made in March 1998, when Israel executed a diplomatic maneuver concerning Security
Council Resolution 425, a document dating back to 1978.
The resolution called for Israel's withdrawal from southern Lebanon, and Israel had always refused to accept it,
arguing that it had no claims in southern Lebanon and
would be happy to leave once the threat to its own security along that border were removed. By accepting the resolution, Israel created some pressure on the Lebanese
government to respond in a way that might lead to Israel's
withdrawal. But this pressure could never be as strong as
Syria's pressure on Lebanon, and this initiative went
nowhere. The net effect has been to reduce the policy debate to the pros and cons of unilateral Israeli withdrawal.

In December 1998 the situation changed again with the
collapse of Netanyahu's coalition. It is moot whether the
prime minister could (and should) have stayed the course
or whether his government was doomed by the tension
between policy (the need to come to an agreement after
nearly two years of procrastination) and politics (the refusal of several right-wing coalition members to support
the government through implementation of the Wye
Agreement). Netanyahu got the Cabinet and the Knesset
to approve the Agreement, but his coalition ran out of
steam soon thereafter. On December 21 the coalition and
opposition joined forces in a vote that dissolved the Knesset and stipulated an early election, called for May 17,
1999, with June 1 as the date for a possible second round
in the prime ministerial election.

During the next few weeks the stage was set for a
lengthy, contentious election campaign. The formation of
a new "center party" meant that for the first time in Is-

rael's political history there would be a three-way race.
Netanyahu and his election advisers chose to focus their
campaign on the peace process and away from socioeconomic issues and from the prime minister's character. The
strategy was to repeat the success of 1996 and to depict
Netanyahu as a resilient, uncompromising leader who, despite the recent Wye Agreement and in contrast to his
meek competitors, would not yield to Arab and, specifically, Palestinian pressures.

Aside from a minor Israeli redeployment and several
meetings of joint committees established by the Wye
Agreement, implementation was suspended in anticipation of the elections. Some protests notwithstanding,
Arafat agreed to this and agreed, in fact, to delay the declaration of Palestine's independence and statehood to the
fall. For one thing, he (and for that matter the Clinton administration) was reluctant to affect the Israeli election
adversely. Whatever their sympathies, each had discovered in 1996 that an overt effort to help Netanyahu's rivals
could backfire; passive communication of one's preferences seemed the safer option. Inasmuch as Arafat was
concerned, this meant that he was not going to overtly
support the Labor candidate, Ehud Barak, or the centrist
Yitzhak Mordechai or be critical of Netanyahu, but like-
wise he was determined not to embarrass Israeli supporters of the peace process by staging a major crisis before
the elections.

In Arafat's strategy, investment in Washington's goodwill
remained cardinal and continued to yield handsome dividends, notably when in mid-December 1998 President
Clinton visited Israel and the Gaza Strip—as agreed on
and announced at the Wye River Conference. The visit

was meant to reinforce the implementation of an agreement that was likely to encounter difficulties. Yasser Arafat and the Palestinians could easily note the political and diplomatic advantages of having the president of the United States visit Gaza, while Netanyahu was promised that Clinton's presence would be used to guarantee a definitive public abrogation of the offensive paragraphs of the Palestinian National Charter. Chairman Arafat registered yet another milestone on his way to Palestinian statehood, and the Israeli prime minister could claim he had obtained the final revision of the document over which he had chided Peres in 1996.

IV

THE WEB OF RELATIONSHIPS

As we have seen throughout this exploration of the Arab-Israeli conflict, the very term is somewhat misleading—implying as it does the notion that a single conflict pits Israel against the Arab world, that the ebb and flow of Israel's relations with the Palestinians are linked organically to, say, its rivalry with Iraq or its complex relationship with Morocco. To a considerable extent this has indeed been true: broad trends have applied across the region; after all, the Arab collective rallied against Israel in 1948, participated in the conflict when it festered and swelled, was devastated by the defeat of 1967, condemned Sadat in 1977 for moving toward peace, and adopted his formula only a decade later. But under the umbrella of unity, there have always been exceptions, rivalries, and tensions within the Arab world.[1]

•   •   •

EGYPT

For the thirty years between its participation in the Arab invasion of the young Jewish state in 1948 and the Camp David Accords of 1978, Egypt was Israel's most formidable foe. Its decision to enter the war in 1948 had not been a matter of course. It was preceded by a policy debate between two principal schools of thought, one upholding the *raison d'état* of the Egyptian state, and the other stressing Egypt's Arab and Islamic commitments, as well as the political imperatives of Egyptian leadership and hegemony.[2] The issue was decided at the eleventh hour by King Farouk, who was motivated by dynastic considerations and personal ambition. His decision's momentous consequences included the monarchy's own downfall four years later, and it added the humiliation of defeat to Egypt's already complex attitude toward Israel.[3]

The 1948 war launched a quarter-century-long cycle of violence that included four full-fledged wars and a war of attrition. On the Egyptian side, the interplay of ideological commitment, state interests, and personal ambition was given new scope and new intensity by the rise of Gamal Abdel Nasser's revolutionary regime. As the leader of a messianic pan-Arab nationalism, as the head of a military regime, as Moscow's ally, and as the president of the Egyptian state, angry at the wedge Israel had driven between Egypt and the eastern Arab world, Nasser mobilized hitherto unfamiliar resources against Israel. Israel viewed Egypt as the key to a peaceful settlement with the Arab world. Yet during most of the Nasserite period the prospect of a settlement seemed remote, and Israel remained deeply concerned that Egypt's power alone was a threat; in addition, it could carry large parts of the Arab world with it. In the May 1967 crisis that deteriorated into the Six-Day War, Egyptian and Israeli misperceptions and misreadings of intentions and capabilities were gross.[4]

Six more years and two more wars were required before Israel and Egypt could move to peaceful settlement and reconciliation, but the foundations for these were laid in the war, in which Israel demonstrated an overwhelming military advantage, acquired territorial assets for a land-for-peace deal, and dealt a devastating blow to Nasser and his regime. When Nasser died in September 1970, his heir apparent, Anwar al-Sadat, was seen by other contenders for power in Egypt as a harmless transitional figure. But Sadat showed himself an astute politician, who outwitted his rivals and emerged as a true international statesman— a dramatic evolution that set the stage for Egypt's reconciliation with Israel.

As part of his comprehensive reorientation of his country's politics and policies, Sadat decided that Egypt must disengage from the conflict with Israel. This agenda and that of Prime Minister Menachem Begin overlapped in 1977 enough to enable them to conclude the Camp David Accords in 1978 and a peace treaty in 1979. For Sadat, peace with Israel was necessary in order to regain the Sinai Peninsula and to build a new relationship with the United States. He was willing to dispute with the other Arab states over his and Egypt's right to follow this policy to give priority to Egypt's own interests over its commitment to the Arab and Palestinian causes. But at no time was Sadat willing to make a separate deal with Israel or to "divorce" his country from its Arab context. Begin, in turn, came to agree to a complete Israeli withdrawal from the

Sinai so as to have peace with this most important Arab
state. But he also presumed that Egypt would willingly acquiesce in a perpetuation of Israel's control of the West
Bank, that somehow the Palestinian autonomy plan that
was part of the peace treaty could be finessed.[5] This certainly was not the Egyptian view of things.

Though implementation of the bilateral part of the
Israeli-Egyptian agreement proceeded smoothly, the collapse of the autonomy negotiations, the continuation of
the Israeli-Palestinian conflict, and Israel's decision to go
to war in Lebanon in 1982 had a very negative effect on
the fledgling peace between Egypt and Israel. This was reinforced by Egyptian considerations—domestic Islamic
opposition and Nasserite criticism, and a desire for reconciliation with the rest of the Arab world. Over the years, as
the result not of a conscious early decision but, rather, of a
murky trial-and-error process, Egypt, first under Sadat
and then under his successor, Hosni Mubarak, adopted a
policy of "cold peace." It kept its principal commitments
toward Israel—diplomatic relations, an agreed-on security
regime in the Sinai, Israeli tourism permitted in Egypt—
but also kept economic and trade relations to a minimum,
discouraged visits by Egyptians to Israel and cultural relations of all kinds, and signaled to the critics of peace with
Israel that the regime did not really frown upon them.
Nor did the government curtail virulent verbal attacks on
Israel and Jews, invoking its commitment to freedom of
the peace.

This policy, which Israel and occasionally the United
States criticized, on the whole functioned reasonably well,
and by the late 1980s Egypt's reconciliation with the Arab
world was completed. With the Soviet Union's decline,

even Sadat's most bitter critic, Hafez al-Assad in Syria, eventually renewed his country's diplomatic relations with Egypt and indicated his readiness to try to resolve its conflict with Israel.

The inauguration of the Madrid process and, even more, the formation of the Rabin-Peres government should have dramatically improved Israeli-Egyptian relations. The separate peace with Israel was now part of a comprehensive peace process; the new Israeli government used Egyptian help to advance its negotiations with the Palestinians, and eventually signed an agreement with them that was much more attractive than the original autonomy plan had been. Yet a real improvement in relations with Egypt failed to happen. It was obviously difficult for Mubarak's regime to dissociate itself from the policy of "cold peace," for it was dealing with a radical Islamic opposition, pursuing an occasionally neo-Nasserist regional and foreign policy, and wanting to signal that it was not Washington's captive. But the additional, larger dimension to Egypt's coolness was its renewed sense of Israel as a competitor. This was given a new urgency by the very success of the peace process. It certainly did not wish to see Israel as a regional superpower enjoying a special relationship with the United States, flexing its military and economic muscles throughout the region and beyond.

There was a time, before the Oslo Accords and for a few months after them, when Egypt appeared reasonably pleased to mediate between Israel and Arab parties. But when Israel signed a peace with Jordan, began to normalize its relations with the Gulf states and in North Africa, and developed new concepts for regional cooperation, this satisfaction was replaced by alarm.[6] And the principal means it used to articulate its unhappiness was the issue of nuclear weapons. Egypt, like the rest of the Arab world, had taken it for granted that Israel had a nuclear arsenal, even though Israel adhered to a policy of studied ambiguity in this matter. For years Israeli governments had been using the convenient formula that "Israel will not be the first nation to introduce nuclear weapons to the Middle East," and had consistently refused to sign the Non-Proliferation Treaty, arguing that it was not willing to undertake its commitments while countries like Iraq and Iran might develop nuclear weapons regardless of having signed the treaty. In the late 1960s, after considerable tension with the United States over this issue, Israel finally arrived at a modus vivendi with Washington; also, its destruction of Iraq's nuclear reactor in 1981 displayed its determination to deny the nuclear option to other Middle Eastern countries.

As the senior Arab state, Egypt traditionally led the Arab world's campaign at the United Nations and elsewhere against Israel's nuclear option. Egypt, as a populous country with a large conventional army, was genuinely opposed to the introduction of nuclear weapons to the Middle East, and resented Israel's quest for nuclear deterrence and nuclear monopoly, considering these as symptoms of Israel's hegemonic and exclusivist ambitions. When the security regime for the Sinai was negotiated at Camp David, Egypt raised questions on this issue and was rebuffed. Sadat chose not to insist so as not to obstruct his main goal—regaining the Sinai. But for the next fifteen years, Egypt continued to raise the issue in the familiar diplomatic settings. When the working group on arms control and regional security (ACRES) began to meet in

1992 (part of the multilateral track of the Madrid process), Egyptian-Israeli disagreements over this issue soon emerged, naturally enough. But by late 1994, a qualitative change had occurred: Egypt began to use the issue in order to slow the diplomacy down—first in ACRES, then in the working group on environmental issues (given the issue of nuclear waste), and finally in the multilateral steering group.

The change was to some extent due to the approaching Non-Proliferation Treaty Review and Extension Conference in April 1995. The United States wanted the treaty to be renewed indefinitely, and to Egypt this seemed like the last opportunity to bring pressure on Israel to sign the treaty. Israel recognized the genuine concern, but it calculated also that Cairo had a much broader agenda: Rabin and Peres could not quite understand why, after fifteen years of passive opposition to Israel's nuclear option, Egypt was shifting to active and vociferous opposition precisely when Arab-Israeli peace seemed to be in reach. As they and their advisers saw it, this was part of a deliberate effort to slow down Israel's "normalization" in the Middle East.

Puzzled and angry as they were, Rabin and Peres chose to moderate their reaction to this Egyptian policy. Israel's relationship with Egypt was too precious and fragile to be guided by emotions. They also understood that when conflict between the two countries ended it would be replaced not by friendship but by peaceful competition. Incidentally, it was convenient for both Egypt and Israel to pretend that Cairo's anti-Israeli moves had been initiated by Foreign Minister Musa, an ambitious man subscribing to a new version of pan-Arabism; this allowed

President Mubarak to stay above the fray as a supreme leader arbitrating between rival factions in his government and nonetheless preserving Egypt's relationship with Israel.[7]

Egypt shared some of Jordan's discomfort with Peres's view of the peace to come, but its criticism was milder, concerned principally with Peres's quest for a new regional order. It was also skeptical of his determination to have Israel come quickly to a far-reaching agreement with Syria, about which Egypt was full of ambiguities. Syria's definition of a "dignified settlement" was expressed in terms that were in contradistinction to the Camp David Accords, and when Syria was discussed as the key to a comprehensive Arab-Israeli settlement, Egypt felt put in second place. But, unlike the Jordanians, the Egyptians still hoped to see Peres win in May 1996, its unhappiness with some aspects of the Labor government's peace policies being minor compared with the prospect of a Netanyahu victory.

Despite Mubarak's open unhappiness with Israel's new prime minister and his policies, a dialogue has been maintained with Netanyahu's government. The Egyptian government has also allowed further degrees of cultural normalization with Israel. Clearly, Mubarak and his aides had come to realize that the policy of cold peace was playing into the hands of the Israeli right wing. At the same time, Egypt took advantage of the political change in Israel to cut the peace process down to size: Egypt does not want this process to transform the regional politics of the Middle East. Having Israel come to a settlement with the Palestinians and eventually with Syria is one thing; watching Israel use these agreements to develop a network of political and economic relations across the Middle East, to construct new strategic relations with Turkey, and to continue special relations with Washington and a nuclear monopoly—that is another.

SYRIA

Relations between Israel and Syria are currently shaped by the legacy of those four and a half years of uncompleted peace negotiation, by lingering rivalry and competition, and by the prospect of renewed conflict. It is hardly surprising that Israel and Syria blame each other for this failure. Most Israelis familiar with the negotiations feel that Assad was genuinely interested in having an agreement; that he wanted to regain the Golan Heights and to build better relations with Washington but continued his ambivalence about reconciliation, let alone normalization, with Israel; and that he was willing to make peace on only very specific terms. Some have argued that he never intended to end with a peace agreement but merely wanted the political dividends deriving from participation in the diplomacy.

Syria's way of telling the story maintains that Yitzhak Shamir never meant to bring the negotiation to a conclusion, that Rabin strung Assad along while he made agreements with the PLO and Jordan and achieved a degree of normalization with other Arab countries and the Arab world in general. According to this version, it was not Assad who failed to take advantage of Peres's willingness to speed up negotiations, but Peres who ruined things by

calling for an early election rather than go along with a negotiation that was finally on the right track.

These issues, described and analyzed in great detail
elsewhere, are overshadowed by another controversy in
present politics and diplomacy. Israel and Syria now
sharply disagree over the legacy and pertinence of the
negotiations, as we have seen.

Yet, through various emissaries, Prime Minister Netanyahu has sent messages to Assad that he thinks seriously about reaching a settlement with Syria. To some
extent this represents a change of policy, but he also has
an apparently genuine fascination with the (unrealistic)
notion of making a deal with Assad quickly, in contrast to
the cumbersome and profoundly controversial Palestinian
talks. The Syrians, conscious of the earlier missed opportunities, would like to resume negotiations, though they
suspect this is either a maneuver designed to play off Syria
and the Palestinians against each other, or a mere attempt
to gain some political points.[8]

In the early and mid-1990s, Syrian, American, and Israeli interlocutors made enormous efforts to persuade
Hafez al-Assad to address the Israeli public, to persuade it
that Syria had gone through a genuine change of heart.
Assad contested the very premises of this effort. As he saw
it, he was not another Sadat, who had to help his Israeli
counterpart build domestic support for making concessions that in his view were mandatory.

The few exercises in public diplomacy to which he
agreed under Washington's pressure were offered grudgingly and proved ineffective and even counterproductive.
Thus, a condolence call by an Israeli Arab delegation after
Assad's son, Basil, was killed in a car accident in January

1994 met, equally, with no response. The United States had persuaded Assad to allow the delegation to enter Syria, making sure that its members did not travel on Israeli passports, arrived by air, and did not come via the Golan. Washington's attempt at goodwill produced in effect yet another manifestation of Syria's only grudging acceptance of the need to come to terms with Israel.[9]

But two recent visits made by Israeli Arabs, some of them active members in Zionist political parties, at Syria's invitation, mark a change; though Assad is still not ready to address the Jewish majority in Israel, he is at least trying to influence part of the Israeli political spectrum.

Beyond the lingering political conflict and diplomatic rivalry lurks the danger of an Israeli-Syrian military clash. This could happen as an unintended consequence of an escalating conflict in Lebanon. If the pressure on Israel continues, not to mention constant Israeli casualties, Israel might resort to more aggressive conduct, which could lead to direct military collision. There are those in Israel who argue that Syria might also decide to break the present deadlock with a limited military operation—the swift capture of a limited piece of territory, say. An immediate cease-fire imposed by the international system would give it victory and possibly set negotiations going that would lead to the return of the Golan Heights to Syria. Much could be argued against this notion, but many in Israel take it seriously. And as the military tension in September 1996 demonstrated, mutual suspicions, groundless as they may be, can lead to an unintended collision.

The suspicions are, indeed, mutual. Most Israelis can hardly envisage their government consciously deciding to go to war against Syria, since victory would be both costly

and pointless. But in Damascus this option is not precluded. As seen from Syria's capital, an Israeli government
headed by an enigmatic prime minister and including two
of the authors of the 1982 war in Lebanon (Ariel Sharon
and Rafael Eytan) is perfectly capable of making such a
decision.

LEBANON

In the 1950s and 1960s, a political cliché was current in Israel to the effect that "Lebanon will be the second Arab
state to sign a peace with Israel." The cliché, clearly not
borne out by the course of events, was inspired by earlier
contacts between Zionist diplomats and some Maronite
Christian leaders in Lebanon and on a mistaken perception of the nature of Lebanese politics. Many Lebanese
Christians thought of Israel as another non-Muslim state
that was or could be a bulwark against pan-Arab nationalism, but most of them viewed Lebanon as part of the Arab
world and wanted to preserve the delicate domestic and
external balances so indispensable to Lebanon's precarious survival.[10]

That balance was upset in the early 1970s, and the
Lebanese state and political system collapsed in the
1975–76 civil war. From Israel's perspective, the civil war
and lingering crisis in Lebanon had several negative results: the Lebanese state was incapable of exercising authority over Lebanese territory, Syria had become the
paramount power and military presence in Lebanon, and
the Palestinians built a territorial base in Beirut and south-

ern Lebanon under PLO direction. Israel responded in various ways: a tactical indirect understanding with Syria to preclude a Syrian military presence in southern Lebanon, an Israeli "security strip" along the Lebanese border, and a strategic alliance with several Maronite groups in Lebanon. But the Lebanese front was the main arena of the PLO's armed conflict with Israel. The growing Palestinian and Syrian challenge and a misguided belief that Israel could place a friendly government in Beirut and change the strategic configuration in the region led Begin's government to launch the 1982 war.

For Lebanon and Israel both, the war had momentous, mostly unintended consequences. The PLO's leaders and troops moved to Tunisia; Syria's hold over Lebanon, after an initial setback, was reinforced; the Christian communities preserved some of their political privileges but lost much power. But the war's single most important outcome was the acceleration of a process that had been apparent earlier—the mobilization of the hitherto underprivileged Shi'ite community and its quest for a political position commensurate with its demographic strength in Lebanon. This trend was reinforced when Iran's Islamic revolution of 1979 was projected into Lebanon and its Shi'ite community—its only successful foreign destination.[11] The Shi'ite militias of Amal and Hizballah were propelled not by nationalism but by religion, and they introduced into the conflict such then-novel elements as suicide bombings.

By 1984, Israel gave up any claim to figure in Lebanon's national politics and focused on the defense of its northern frontier. It withdrew to an expanded security zone maintained by the Israeli Defense Force with the help of

a local militia; since then, the security zone and occasionally Israel itself have been attacked primarily by Hizballah,
under direction from Teheran and with the tacit cooperation of Syria.

In October 1989, an Arab conference held in Taif, in
Saudi Arabia, tried to consolidate and formalize the situation. The compromise embodied in the Taif accord envisaged Syria's military withdrawal from Lebanon, albeit as a
remote prospect. But the accord remained a dead letter.
In fact, Syria took advantage of its participation in the
American-led coalition during the Gulf crisis and Gulf
War to consolidate its hold over Lebanon; fourteen years
after its original invasion, Syria finally controlled Lebanon
through a functioning local government, maintaining a significant military presence in there not as an army of occupation but as a guarantor of its hegemony, as a defender of
the western approaches to Damascus, and as a potential
threat to Israel. Syria makes a point of acting as the
guardian of the trappings of Lebanese statehood, but in
subtle and less-than-subtle ways it ensures Lebanon's acquiescence with its will and interests. Thus, no progress
should be made in Lebanese-Israeli negotiations so long
as a breakthrough has not occurred in Syrian-Israeli relations; Syria has undertaken, once such a breakthrough oc-
curs, to obtain a comparable agreement for Lebanon; and
Lebanon's territory must be used to pressure Israel to
come to terms with Syria.

In 1994, the broad lines of an understanding about
Lebanon were, in fact, worked out between Israel and
Syria in the "ambassadors' channel." Provided that a
Syrian-Israeli agreement was reached, Syria was willing to
endorse an Israeli-Lebanese peace agreement to be im-

plemented within nine months—a time frame that coincided with the nine months that Rabin envisaged for the first phase of a prospective agreement with Syria. But no such agreement was reached.

Unfortunately, there was also a violent side to this story. Hizballah's offensive against Israel's security zone in southern Lebanon and occasional Katyusha rocket attacks on northern Israel kept up a permanent cycle of violence along the Lebanese-Israeli border. Twice—in July 1993 and April 1996—Israel launched large-scale land operations in Lebanon in an effort to break the cycle. Both operations led to "understandings" between Israel and Hizballah that limited the violence but failed to end it.

Soon after the formation of his government in June 1996, Netanyahu sought to promote a "Lebanon First" initiative, which he hoped would win Syrian endorsement. But Syria suspected this was an attempt to drive a wedge between Damascus and Beirut, and it wasted no time in rebuffing the gambit. In September, a redeployment of Syrian troops in Lebanon led to a brief war-scare, since some in Israel wrongly interpreted it as a preparation for launching an attack, while Syrians wrongly interpreted Israel's statements and responsive movements as preparations for an attack. Eventually, reassuring messages were exchanged and a confrontation was averted, but the episode showed how explosive the Israeli-Syrian-Lebanese triangle was.

As the months have gone by and the number of Israeli casualties has grown dramatically, so has public and political pressure to extricate Israeli soldiers from southern Lebanon. A mixed coalition of concerned parents, left-wing politicians, and Golan settlers who are eager to sever

the link between southern Lebanon and the Golan
Heights has led a movement calling for Israel's unilateral
withdrawal from Lebanon. Netanyahu's government responded with a novel tactic—a conditional acceptance of
Security Council Resolution 425, requiring Israel to leave
Lebanon. This put Lebanon's President Hirawi and Prime
Minister Hariri in a difficult position: it was hard for them
to explain why they were refusing to take Israel up on its
offer to withdraw. Their predicament enhanced Syria's
suspicions that they might seek accommodation with Israel on their own, and Syria made highly visible efforts to
keep Lebanon's government in tow.

JORDAN

Israel shares its longest border with Jordan; the two countries have immense actual and potential impact on each
other's national security and economy, but their relationship is, and for a long time has been, primarily affected
by their respective and common relations with a third
party—the Palestinians.

Jordan's very birth as a modern state was intimately
linked to this issue. When Great Britain decided in 1921
to create *ex nihilo* a principality for the Hashemite
monarch Amir Abdullah, it needed to placate him personally and the Hashemite family in general for what they
considered a betrayal—for their receiving only a meager
share in the postwar settlement in the Middle East—and
so it detached the East Bank from the territory of Mandate Palestine and gave it to Jordan. In doing so, Britain

was also trying to reduce the impact that the formation of a Jewish national home in Palestine would have on the region. During the next twenty-five years, Abdullah, with British help, developed a genuine polity in Jordan, and in 1946 the principality became a kingdom. At the same time, a significant political relationship grew between Abdullah and the leaders of the Jewish community in pre-state Israel, the Yishuv. This understanding was predicated on their common enmity to radical Palestinian Arab nationalism, as personified by Haj Amin al-Husayni, mufti of Jerusalem. Abdullah was hostile not merely to the mufti but to his political style and to the brand of Arab nationalism that he represented. And he was never satisfied with the desert principality assigned to him and was eager to extend his rule to more significant territories and cities—Syria and Damascus, or Palestine west of the Jordan and Jerusalem.

When the idea of partitioning Palestine into Jewish and Arab states came to the fore in 1937, a new dimension was added to Abdullah's relationship with the Yishuv. If this partition came to pass, he might annex the Arab part of Palestine to his kingdom and provide the stability and pragmatism that had been so glaringly absent from the scene. The term "Jordanian option" was coined later, but the concept originated then: the solution of Israel's Palestinian dilemma by means of Jordan. This became a viable option after the UN's partition resolution of November 1947.

The Jewish leaders had accepted the notion of Palestine's partition and were quite content to go along with part of Abdullah's annexation plan. But they disliked the other aspect of Abdullah's policy—his part in the Arab states' invasion of Palestine on May 15, 1948, which would facilitate his own takeover of the area assigned to be a Palestinian-Arab state in the partition plan.

During the war, Abdullah's army, the Arab Legion, was a resolute and effective enemy that inflicted on the young Israeli Defense Force some of its most painful defeats, and at the war's end Abdullah was indeed in control of what became known as the West Bank and East Jerusalem. His annexation of these territories was formally recognized by only two foreign governments, but, whatever the legal aspects, it transformed the Jordanian polity. (It was called Transjordan until 1964, and Jordan thereafter.) Palestinians now made up a majority of its population; many of them regarded Abdullah, his kingdom, and his act of annexation as illegitimate.[12] And in the years before Abdullah was assassinated by a Palestinian in 1951, the transformation of his kingdom's traditional politics as a consequence of the annexation of this large, better-educated, politically mobilized, and embittered Palestinian population had become apparent. In 1949–50, a treaty between Israel and Jordan was negotiated and initialed but it was not finalized, for Abdullah realized that he had neither the power nor the authority to carry his country with him to a peace settlement with Israel.[13]

During the next fifteen years, the issue was not annexation but survival. Following a brief regency period, the eighteen-year-old Hussein ascended the throne which he was to occupy for forty-five years. The young monarch proved to be extremely determined, astute in maintaining external support and facing down domestic opposition, and unusually skillful and lucky at aborting plots and evading assassination attempts. For revolutionary Arab nationalism held sway over much of the Middle East, and the king's Palestinian subjects were among its staunchest supporters. Yet at the same time Jordan, reflecting the new demographic realities and in keeping with its claim to embody the Palestinian issue, was the only Arab state that offered citizenship to Palestinians. In 1967, King Hussein paid dearly when he joined Egypt and Syria in their war against Israel, and he lost the West Bank and Jerusalem. Jordan now had no West Bank but a Palestinian majority in the East Bank; yet by then many Palestinians had been "Jordanized" and had come to accept Jordan as their country and state. Yearning for Palestinian self-determination is one thing, and the realization that life under the Hashemites is quite attractive is another.[14]

So the Six-Day War reopened "the question of Palestine." For the first time since 1948, all of what had been Mandate Palestine was placed under a single authority. Israel was in control of the sizable Palestinian population living in the West Bank and in the Gaza Strip, in addition to its own Palestinian Arab minority. The debate over the future of the West Bank and the Gaza Strip became the governing issue of Israeli politics. For Israel, three principal alternatives presented themselves: reviving the "Jordanian option"; seeking or accepting the creation of an independent or autonomous Palestinian entity; or perpetuating Israeli control, either as a deliberate policy or, more likely, by failing to make painful choices.

The Hashemite regime's initial preference was to come to an agreement with Israel, but the king insisted that he could only do so on the basis of Israel's full withdrawal from the occupied territories. With the passage of time, as Israel's attachment to the West Bank grew stronger and so did the PLO's stature and power, the prospects for this "Jordanian option" waned. Nor did various notions of a Jordanian-Palestinian federation turn into a magic formula.

Its protestations of formal support notwithstanding, Jordan has consistently opposed or at least been uneasy about the idea of a Palestinian state in the West Bank and the Gaza Strip. For Hashemite Jordan, a small Palestinian state in part of the West Bank and the Gaza Strip cannot be a durable, satisfactory solution to the Palestinian problem, and Palestinians are likely to direct their irredentist claims eastward and to seek the allegiance of Jordan's Palestinian majority. True, many of the kingdom's Palestinian subjects view themselves as Jordanians, but why expose their loyalty to such a challenge?[15] So, for many long years, staying with the status quo proved to be the easiest choice for Jordan, too. A channel of communication with the Israeli leadership was kept discreetly open, but not quite secret, for nearly three decades. Several attempts were made to reach a settlement, various practical issues were sorted out, and a dialogue was maintained between King Hussein and most of Israel's prime ministers. A community of interests was established with both Labor and Likud leaders, based on shared opposition to the PLO and to the notion of Palestinian statehood.

One tenet of this relationship—the Israeli belief that the survival of the Hashemite regime and its control of the East Bank were important Israeli national interests—was shaken when, in 1970, Likud adopted the slogan "Jordan is Palestine" and took the position that there was no need to establish a second Palestinian state. The argument also presumed that, once the Palestinians took over the reins of government in Amman, their claim over the West Bank would weaken.[16] The issue came into stark relief in September, when Israel was key in facilitating King Hussein's victory over Syria and the PLO. Golda Meir and Yitzhak Rabin believed that his survival and American-Israeli strategic cooperation should be Israel's paramount considerations; their decision was subsequently criticized by Ariel Sharon, leader of Israel's radical right, who argued that the government had missed an opportunity "to let nature take its course."

In the rich chronology of Israeli-Jordanian history during these years, several defining events stand out: King Hussein's decision not to join the Arab war coalition in October 1973; Kissinger's inability to effect an Israeli-Jordanian interim agreement in the spring of 1974; the Arab summit's decision in October 1974 to designate the PLO as the legitimate claimant to the West Bank; the London Agreement of April 1987, which was Israel's last attempt to exercise the "Jordanian option," albeit in a modified version; Jordan's formal disengagement from the West Bank in 1988;* and the Gulf crisis and Gulf War, which was the culmination of Iraq's threat to Jordan's independence.

The signing of the Oslo Accords affected this history paradoxically. The Hashemites resented Israel's choice of a "Palestinian option," but decided that they had to draw closer to Israel, the better to affect the course of events. The emergence of a Palestinian state, though it became

---

*It is significant that, though King Hussein publicly announced his country's disengagement, the formal annexation act was never abrogated, nor has Jordan's constitution been amended. It still stipulates that the "territory [of the kingdom] is indivisible and no portion of it may be ceded."[17]

more likely, was not a foregone conclusion, and Jordan and Israel still shared a significant agenda. But there was another side to the same developments. By signing the Oslo Accords with Israel, the PLO enabled Jordan and other Arab states to pursue their bilateral agendas with Israel. But at issue was a trilateral relationship, for the United States was involved; there were also regional issues (strategic cooperation with Turkey, the future of Iraq).

Meanwhile, Israel's commitment to the survival of King Hussein's regime was buttressed by a close personal relationship between King Hussein and Yitzhak Rabin. This changed during Peres's brief tenure as Rabin's successor. The king was worried that his policies would lead all too quickly to an independent Palestinian state and to Israeli-Syrian and Syrian-Lebanese agreements; these would jeopardize and dwarf Jordan's position. On the eve of the May 1996 elections, Jordan indicated its preference for Benjamin Netanyahu and a peace policy managed at a more deliberate pace.

Yet these hopes were not fulfilled. For, although Jordan is opposed to an accelerated peace process, it finds it essential to have a viable one, particularly vis-à-vis the Palestinians. The collapse of Israeli-Palestinian negotiations, let alone outbreaks of Israeli-Palestinian violence, would make Jordan's peace with Israel hardly tenable. This may be a tall order, but the Hashemites expect from Israel finesse and subtlety in the conduct of a delicate, fragile relationship. They soon came to believe that Netanyahu was a prime minister who could not manage that relationship, who could not keep the king's personal trust, and whose real intentions with regard to the peace process could not be divined. The king vented his frustration in a scathing letter to Netanyahu, the text of which became available to the international media. Yet the king kept the lid on: most of the interests that keep Jordan wanting a peace with Israel are still valid, and the cost of an open break with Israel still outweighs the benefits it might produce. And so, for the time being, Israeli-Jordanian peace has survived, but the expectations of a special relationship, a warm peace, and a mutually beneficial web of economic and development projects has failed to materialize.

In February 1999, King Hussein died of the cancer he had fought during the previous few years. On his deathbed he removed his brother Hassan, who had served as crown prince for more than thirty years, and appointed his oldest son, Abdullah, as his heir. After ascending the throne, the young king reassured Israel on several occasions that he was committed to the peace his father had signed. Yet Israeli apprehensions about Jordan's ability to contend with potential and external threats were exacerbated by the simultaneous loss of two experienced and familiar partners.

THE PALESTINIANS

In October 1975, a senior American Arabist, Harold Saunders, testified at a hearing held by the House of Representatives' Committee on Foreign Affairs. In his prepared written text, Saunders referred to the Palestinian issue as the core of the conflict between Arabs and Israelis in the Middle East.[18] At the time, little attention was paid to Saunders's testimony, but it subsequently drew considerable attention and animated objections from the Israeli government. Israel was then in the midst of a complex diplomatic process orchestrated by the United States and predicated on the assumption that the key to the Arab-Israeli conflict lay in Israel's relations with the major Arab states. Saunders's argument ran against the grain of U.S.-Israeli policies and was, indeed, a harbinger of the change that came with the Carter presidency. If the Palestinian issue was the core question of the Arab-Israeli conflict, did it not make sense to predicate the quest for Arab-Israeli peace on a resolution of the problem that lay at its heart? Indeed, the Carter administration, and Saunders, acted in the Middle East on the dual assumption that it could resolve the Palestinian problem and that its success would offer the key to a comprehensive Arab-Israeli peace.

But was such a resolution feasible? Since 1948, Israeli attitudes toward Palestinians have to a large extent been shaped by a sense that the Israeli-Palestinian dispute is a zero-sum game, that Palestinian demands and expectations can be met only by intolerable terms. It was much easier for Israel and Israelis to think of Israeli-Arab reconciliation by means of negotiations and agreements with states like Egypt, Jordan, and Syria, which could focus on such issues as boundaries and water.[19]

This frame of mind was for many years reinforced by the course of Palestinian history and the drift of Palestinian politics. Between 1949 and 1964, the Palestinians were absent from the Middle Eastern arena as an independent force. They were crushed, fragmented, and dispersed. Their traditional leaders were discredited, and most young Palestinian activists invested their zeal in ideological parties that promised a remedy to the Palestinian predica-

THE WEB OF RELATIONSHIPS

ment within a larger scheme. The Arab states, in turn, were eager to take charge of the Palestinian issue and to suppress the efforts made by Palestinian groups to take charge themselves. For more than a decade, the vast majority of them were under the spell of Gamal Abdel Nasser and his brand of messianic pan-Arab nationalism. When Nasser defeated the enemy—the unholy trinity of Western imperialism, Zionism, and domestic reactionary forces—and united the Arab homeland, Arab Palestine would be liberated and redeemed. It was only with Nasser's and Nasserism's decline that an authentic Palestinian national movement was born.

The PLO was founded by the Arab states as their instrument but was taken over in 1968 by the authentic Palestinian groups that had emerged a few years earlier. Yet, for another twenty-five years, most Israelis did not consider the PLO an acceptable interlocutor. It had drafted a charter that called for Israel's destruction, and it used terror as a principal instrument. All efforts to persuade Arafat to take positions that would enable the PLO to join the peace process in the 1970s were to no avail. The PLO only slowly adopted the formula of a "two-state solution." Nor was Israel, the more powerful party to the conflict, ready or willing to take the initiative.[20]

Thus, while Israel and Egypt went ahead toward their peace treaty of 1979, armed conflict between Israel and Palestinian nationalists and their struggle over the land of the West Bank continued. The ambivalence and equivocation that marked Israel's Labor governments about putting Jewish settlements in the West Bank was replaced after the Likud victory in 1977 with open encouragement to do so. These efforts created (mostly by design) a new reality

under which a workable compromise with the Palestinians
became ever more difficult to achieve, yet at the same
time the sight of expanding Israeli settlements persuaded
many Palestinians, particularly in the West Bank and the
Gaza Strip, that time was not necessarily on their side and
that it was imperative to reach a settlement.

In 1988, Arafat finally endorsed the principle of a two-
state solution and on that basis diplomacy began between
the PLO and the United States. The changes in Washington's and the PLO's positions amplified the considerable
impact of the *intifada*, and increased the pressure on Israel's second national-unity government to renew, after a
seven-year hiatus, negotiations about Palestinian self-rule.
The profound disagreement between the government's
Labor and Likud components over this issue expedited its
collapse in March 1990. When Israeli-Palestinian negotiations began again in 1991, they were part of the Madrid
process, and they played out against the backdrop of other
great changes: the Soviet Union's collapse, the end of the
Cold War, the Gulf crisis and Gulf War, and a fresh wave
of emigrants from the former Soviet Union to Israel.

In the course of putting the Madrid process together,
Secretary of State Baker discovered that Prime Minister
Shamir's resistance to the very notion of negotiating with
the Palestinians could be mitigated by shifting the emphasis from the Palestinian issue to having a parallel channel
of diplomacy with Israel's Arab neighbors. This blunted
the Palestinian edge of the Madrid process, which was
further reduced by the formal incorporation of the Palestinian delegation into a Jordanian-Palestinian delegation.
But the junior status thus assigned to the Palestinians, and
the PLO's formal absence from the Madrid process, re-

flected the PLO's decline in the Arab world after the Gulf War, though the effect of this humiliating turn of events was limited at first, since no progress occurred during the first nine months of the post-Madrid negotiations. But when the Rabin government was formed, the PLO's hold over Palestinian politics acquired fresh significance. An Israeli-Palestinian agreement became a key to any progress; whether Israel would come to such an agreement without the PLO or deal with the PLO and find an acceptable formula became a crucial issue on its diplomatic agenda.

We have seen how Rabin pondered the comparative advantages of the Syrian and Palestinian options. In early August 1993, the hypothetical vacillation turned into an actual policy choice. Then, by signing the Oslo Accords, Israel predicated the new phase of the peace process on its agreement with the PLO, and not with a major Arab state such as Syria. This resulted in a radical change of perspective. Having signed a framework agreement with representatives of Palestinian nationalism, Israel now argued that the core issue of the Arab-Israeli conflict had been addressed and the chief obstacle to Arab-Israeli reconciliation and normalization had been removed. This created a hitherto unfamiliar mutual dependence between the government of Israel and the PLO leaders.

The Oslo process was a very complex and fragile mechanism; genuine cooperation and a genuine sense of partnership were indispensable to its success. As we have seen, these were accomplished to only a limited degree.

And the Israeli-Palestinian conflict was not over. In both societies, powerful forces were opposed to reconciliation and continued to try to abort it. Competition for

control of the West Bank and Jerusalem continued, and
the leaders, cooperating as they did in implementing the
agreements they had signed, were separated by their different visions of the final-status agreement. Both societies
had yet to think through, separately or together, some fundamental issues. Were Israel and the Palestinians interested in separation, or in some form of cooperation or
integration within the Israeli-Jordanian-Palestinian triangle? And if separation was what they wanted, was it feasible? And what sort of a relationship could be envisaged
between societies separated by such social and economic
gaps? How would twelve or fifteen million Israelis and
Arabs share the limited resources of land and water in the
space between the Mediterranean and the Jordan early in
the next century?

FROM "ISRAELI ARABS" TO
"ISRAEL'S PALESTINIAN CITIZENS"

In the original terminology of the Arab-Israeli dispute, the
conflict in and over British Mandate Palestine was conducted between an Arab side and a Jewish side. It was
only after the establishment of the state of Israel and the
conclusion of the 1948 war that a stark distinction was
drawn between Israelis and Palestinians as the successors
of the Jewish and Arab communities in Palestine. In Israeli usage, the term "Arab" came to refer to the people
who lived in the larger Arab world beyond Israel's borders,
while the term "Palestinian" referred to Palestinians resid-
ing outside Israel. Israel's own Arab or Palestinian citizens

were strictly referred to as "Israeli Arabs," as members of Israel's "Arab minority" or "sector." This curious choice of terms well expressed Israelis' uneasiness about the Palestinian issue. It was, in a way, easier to cope with a national minority pertaining to an amorphous Arab world than with a people who laid specific claim to Israel's own land.[21] For twenty years or so, Israel's Arab citizens accepted this terminology and used it themselves, but by the 1970s they began to refer to themselves as Palestinians or as Palestinians who happened to be Israeli citizens. This was but one of many profound changes in the complex relationship between the Israeli state and its Arab citizens.

When the 1948 war ended, some 130,000 Palestinian Arabs remained in the territory of the independent Jewish state and became its citizens. So the fledgling state of Israel had a population of just over a million, and its Arab citizens constituted a minority of about 11 percent. In the aftermath of a brutal war, the victorious Jews considered this Arab minority as a potential fifth column, liable to be used by a hostile Arab world in an inevitable, imminent "second round." This underlying attitude was translated into a policy of control embodied first and foremost by the imposition of a system of "military government" on the Arab population, which was abolished only in 1966 by Israel's third prime minister, Levi Eshkol.

This policy of control was carried out in an ambivalent context. Israel as a Jewish state was hard put to decide whether it wanted to separate the Arab minority from the mainstream of Israeli public life or whether, as a democratic state dominated by a social-democratic political establishment, to integrate it. Ironically, integration was first accomplished, after a fashion, in the political realm. As full-fledged citizens of the state of Israel (though not equal members of Israel's body politic and society), most Israeli Arabs voted for Zionist parties through satellite lists and in fact helped to perpetuate Labor's hegemony.

During these early years, the Arab minority, predominantly rural and Muslim, can best be described as powerless, traumatized, and confused. Its members had to adjust to defeat, to minority status, to isolation from the other parts of the fragmented Palestinian community, and from the larger Arab world. And there was an acute problem of leadership—the pre-1948 Palestinian Arab elites were now beyond Israel's borders, and those who had stayed tended to be poorer and less educated. Arab political opinion and activity in Israel spanned a spectrum that went from pragmatic acceptance of the reality of the Jewish state to nationalist opposition to and rejection of it. Pragmatism was manifested by most Arabs' voting for the major Zionist parties, and opposition was manifested primarily through the Communist Party. Attempts to form a local Arab nationalist party (notably a grouping called Al-Ard, "The Land") collapsed when faced with an insurmountable obstacle: in order to qualify as such, the party would adopt a platform negating Israel's very existence and legitimacy as a Jewish state, and then the government and courts would label it seditious. A subtler, politically easier way for members of the intellectual Arab elite in Israel to express their rejection of the Israeli state was in literary prose and verse.

As in so many other respects, 1967 was a watershed in the evolution of Israel's Arab minority. The re-emergence of an authentic and effective Palestinian nationalist movement and the removal of the physical barrier that had once separated them from the Palestinian and Arab worlds beyond Israel's borders induced a process of Palestinization. But the balance that had been achieved in practice between Israeli and Arab nationalist components in the community was upset. It was a measure of this change that the term "Israeli Arab" was discarded, and Israel's Arab citizens came to refer to themselves as Palestinians. This nationalist awakening, coupled with socioeconomic improvements—a higher standard of living, a higher level of education, the partial breakdown of the extended-family system, the transformation of several villages into towns—led to a new phase of political activism. On March 30, 1976, a massive protest was organized under the title "The Day of the Land" against the expropriation of Arab-owned land in the Galilee. In clashes with security forces, six people were killed. March 30 became an annual day of protest for Palestinians in Israel and in the West Bank and Gaza.

Yasser Arafat and the PLO turned "The Day of the Land" into an all-Palestinian event, but as a rule the PLO did not view Israel's Arab minority as part of its constituency. Long before the PLO formally accepted the notion of a two-state solution, its leaders had presumed it, while the Arabs in Israel, though galvanized by Palestinian nationalism, continued to see their future within the state of Israel. Some Israeli Arabs crossed a physical and mental line and joined the PLO and its orbit, but the vast majority continued to live within the Israeli state and system. Israel's Arab minority did not join either the violent conflicts between the PLO and Israel or the *intifada*.

Still, the patterns of organization and activity in Israeli Arab political life after 1967 underwent profound changes. The Zionist parties' satellite lists disappeared, and nationalist Arab parties were formed that found a way of operating within the boundaries of Israeli law (most notably Abdel Wahab Darawshe's Arab Democratic Party, founded in 1988). Semi-political civic groups like the Committee of Heads of Local Arab Councils emerged. In the late 1970s, a powerful fundamentalist movement appeared, partly as a reflection of regional trends and partly in response to particular local conditions. Muslim fundamentalists in Israel are primarily a religious and social phenomenon, but their potential political power is enormous.[22]

The Oslo and Washington Accords of 1993 were another watershed. On the one hand, the agreement between and mutual recognition of the state of Israel and the Palestinian national movement released Israel's Arab citizens, as it did other Arabs, from their all-embracing commitment to the Palestinian cause and enabled them to pursue their particular causes and interests. Most Arabs living in Israel now consider themselves Palestinians and support the ideas of Palestinian self-determination and statehood, but they are not interested in becoming part of that state. Rather, they view themselves as a Palestinian component of Israel and are primarily interested in their status and position within its systems. For Israel, encumbered with difficult problems of segmentation and coping with contending definitions of its political community, the Arab minority's new focus on its relationship with the state is not easy. Nor is the challenge alleviated by the diversity of Arab opinion. Most Arab citizens of Israel care about the mundane issues of integration and equality—educational opportunities, a larger slice of the national economic pie. But the intellectual and political elites address and challenge the very foundations of the Israeli state and system as presently constituted. Some demand that Israel "de-Zionize" itself and become "a state for all its citizens," or, in other words, cease to define and conduct itself as the national state of the Jewish people and become a state in which Arabs can be full members of the political community, rather than members of a national minority with less than full civil and political rights. Others speak of autonomy or a return to the old notion of a "binational state."

Such ideas are amplified by their converging with a "post-Zionist" ideology that has been adopted by parts of the Israeli left. Whether they argue that Zionism was or is inherently wrong, or whether they feel that Zionism has accomplished its original mission and should change, they, too, advocate a reformulation of the underlying ethos of the Israeli polity, and commensurate constitutional and political changes.[23]

But of far greater potential significance is the growing Arab vote in Israeli politics. At the end of 1996, there were 1,122,000 non-Jews in Israel, 19.5 percent of the total population. (This figure includes 180,000 Palestinian residents of East Jerusalem, who were annexed to Israel but have chosen not to vote in Israeli elections, and 50,000 non-Arab Christians. If these two figures are subtracted, there remain 900,000 Arab citizens of pre-1967 Israel, constituting 15.5 percent of the general population.) The present Knesset has 12 Arab members out of 120. Four of them were elected from Zionist lists (3 in the Labor Party's list and 1 through the left-wing Meretz) and 8 through Arab, non- or anti-Zionist ones. (Formally speaking, the New Communist List is a nonsectarian Arab-

Jewish party; it has Jewish members and activists, and sent one Jewish member to the Knesset, but essentially it is an Arab party.) It is also important to look at the breakdown of Arab votes for Knesset members in 1992 and 1996:

	1992	1996
	(in percentage of Arab voters)	
Democratic Front for Peace and Equality	23.2	37.0
Unified Arab List (Arab Democratic Party and Islamists)	15.2	25.4

		1992	1996	
Labor		20.3	16.6	
Meretz		9.7	10.5	
Likud and (Jewish)	61.6 {			} 37.6
Religious Parties		19.3	5.2	
Others		12.3	5.3	

The change is striking. In 1992, a clear majority of Israel's Arabs voted for mainstream Zionist parties, and less than 40 percent voted for non- or anti-Zionist Arab lists. In 1996, the figures were reversed.

In weighing the significance of this change, it is important to consider the effect of the electoral system introduced in the 1996 elections. Like other groups in the Israeli electorate that could now split their vote, Arab voters tended to cast their "responsible" ballots for the prime minister's post and to "go ethnic" with their party-list ballots. So Arab voters gave overwhelming support to Peres against Netanyahu but drifted away from Zionist party lists to Arab nationalist ones when voting for local candidates.

But the change in the electoral system clearly accelerated trends that had been set in motion much earlier.

The full impact of these trends has thus far been blunted by the fragmentation of the Arab vote, but the importance of the Arab vote and of Arab politicians and groups to Israeli politics is bound to increase dramatically in the coming years. In a deeply divided political system, in which national elections are often decided by only two or three percentage points, the Arab vote can become decisive. And when it is, vociferous complaints by the Jewish nationalist right wing will follow, for this group views the Arab vote as less than fully legitimate. The argument was raised in the early 1990s that the Rabin and Peres governments, relying as they did on the votes of Arab members of the Knesset, did not have a "Jewish majority." In the 1996 elections, Netanyahu defeated Peres by the slim edge of only some sixteen thousand votes, but Netanyahu had a clear majority of 55 percent among Jewish voters. Had Peres squeaked in, the right wing would probably have complained that he had been elected by "the Arab vote" and had no mandate to make concessions unacceptable to "the Jewish majority."

ISRAEL AND IRAQ:
CONFLICT WITHOUT RELATIONS

Iraq occupies a special place among all of Israel's relationships with Arab nations. Iraq is sufficiently remote from Israel to have chosen to act as a "nonconfrontation" state, but for a variety of reasons its rulers have preferred over the years to participate in military conflict with Israel even though it does not share a border with Israel. Indeed, the absence of a common border has radicalized the Iraqi-Israeli conflict. Arab-Israeli peace has mostly been predicated on these two foundations—that the cost of war is prohibitive and that "land" can be exchanged for "peace." Neither is an element in the Israeli-Iraqi equation, and the conflict between the two countries has been nourished by other sources.

The pattern was established early. Iraq played an important part in the 1948 war, by pushing for Arab participation and by sending an expeditionary force to it. But, unlike Israel's immediate neighbors, Iraq chose not to end with an armistice agreement, and in similar fashion it dispatched expeditionary forces in 1967 and 1973 but took no part in the diplomatic activities that brought these wars to an end.[24]

Israel's conflict with the conservative Iraqi regime of the decade after the 1948 war was muted. But the overthrow of the Iraqi monarchy and its replacement by a succession of revolutionary and post-revolutionary regimes changed the situation. Showing their own ambitions for Arab leadership and their competition with Egypt and Syria, Iraq's leaders from Qassem to Saddam Hussein tended to take the most radical positions and to pursue them from the comparative safety afforded by distance. Israel, in turn, was worried by the prospect of having to confront Iraq's full potential as a participant in future wars, as the linchpin of an eastern front comprising Iraq, Syria, and Jordan, or as an immediate neighbor if it took over Jordan. To keep such possibilities at bay, Israel pursued two principal policies: it helped the Kurdish secessionists in northern

Iraq, and it cultivated a strategic alliance with the Shah's Iran. (This latter had a broader agenda, but common enmity with Iraq was an important component.) These Israeli actions, needless to say, were well known to the Iraqis and helped to develop further their view of Israel as a dangerous national enemy.[25]

This configuration was altered in the late 1970s, when the peace treaty with Israel was signed, when Israel lost its alliance with Iran, and when the Kurdish rebellion collapsed. Saddam Hussein's rise to power thus ushered in a period of domestic stability. Over time, Saddam built an army of sixty(!) divisions and also sought to obtain nuclear weapons and other weapons of mass destruction. Along with Hafez al-Assad, Saddam led the opposition to Sadat and Egyptian-Israeli peace, but he and his country were soon absorbed in Iraq's eight-year war with Iran.[26] Israel was worried not so much about Iraq's conventional military buildup as about its acquisition and development of weapons of mass destruction—chemical weapons, Scud missiles, and, most ominously, nuclear weapons. Israel was not necessarily the only likely target: Saddam's army used chemical weapons against Kurdish civilians, and Scud missiles were launched against Iran. But the notion that a regime like Saddam Hussein's might be in possession of nuclear weapons was unacceptable. When, in May 1981, an Israeli air raid destroyed Ossirak, Iraq's nuclear reactor, Iraq did not respond or retaliate, but Israel's action further exacerbated Iraq's hostility.[27]

The end of the war against Iraq had the effect of releasing the huge military machine that Saddam Hussein had constructed. He was determined to use it in order to aggrandize his regime, and he saw Israel as a principal foe

and an obstacle to his schemes. In April 1990, he publicly
warned that Iraq possessed "binary chemical weapons"
and threatened to "make fire eat up half of Israel if it tries
to do anything against Iraq." He may have been thinking
of the conquest of Kuwait, or of Israel's anticipated opposition to any Iraqi act of aggrandizement, but he was also
trying to deter Israel from interfering with his plans, and
to couch his expansionist schemes in anti-Israeli terms.[28]
In the event, Saddam chose to carry out his aggrandizement in the Gulf; he occupied Kuwait and threatened
Saudi Arabia, thus triggering the crisis of 1990 and the war
of 1991. He positioned himself as a latter-day Nasser fighting for the Arab cause against the West and against Israel,
depicting his occupation of Kuwait as part of a broader
challenge to the colonial order that had been imposed on
the Arab world at the end of World War I. This was hollow
posturing, and most of the Arab world saw it as such. But
some mistakenly either accepted Saddam's claims or believed that he would somehow emerge victorious. The
PLO's leaders and many Palestinians in the Gulf made
these errors.[29]

During the Gulf War, Saddam fired about forty Scud
missiles at Israel, primarily in order to draw Israel into the
war and to split the Arab coalition the United States had
organized against him. Shamir's government, partly of its
own volition and partly under American pressure, did not
respond—restraint that paid off handsomely. The U.S.-led
coalition decimated Iraq's military machine, and the con-
straints imposed on Iraq by the United States through
the UN at the war's end destroyed almost all, if not all, of
Iraq's missiles and unconventional arsenal; a sanctions
regime severely limited Iraq's oil exports and oil revenues.

Washington's "containment" of Iraq has denied it any effective role in the Middle East since 1991.

In the 1980s, at the height of its war with Iran, and then in the 1990s, Iraq sent some indirect messages to Israel that it was interested in entering into a tacit dialogue. Some Israeli politicians and strategic planners supported this idea, arguing that it could balance the threat posed by Iran or provide leverage vis-à-vis Syria. Others argued that Saddam was not credible, that Israel should support U.S. policy and not subvert it, and that in any event Iraq was not seriously interested in dialogue but, at best, in buying some goodwill in the United States. The latter arguments prevailed, and a tacit dialogue, whether or not Saddam intended it, never developed.

Israel, alongside the United States, monitors closely Iraq's compliance with the regulations imposed on Baghdad at the end of the Gulf War. With almost all of Iraq's arsenal of weapons of mass destruction and ballistic missiles destroyed, as well as its capacity to reproduce them, and with Iraq's oil exports limited to the bare minimum, this edge of Iraq's offensive capabilities has been blunted. Saddam's limited resources have been invested instead in his regime's very survival. But he has also been remarkably consistent in his drive to erode this situation, to corrode Middle Eastern and international support for Washington's policies, and to maintain or restore at least a measure of Iraq's offensive capability. On several occasions the United States responded to these challenges with limited military action and in February 1998 prepared the ground for a large-scale operation. The arrangement worked out in 1997 is precarious, and a crisis could easily re-erupt.

Israel has an ambivalent view on these developments. It

has an obvious vested interest in Washington's policy, but it is also aware of the increasing boldness of Saddam's challenge. During the crisis of February 1998 the possibility that Iraq might have kept several Scud missiles to use against Israel in the event of an American attack sufficed to create a war scare of sorts. This failed to take place, and the Clinton administration settled instead on a series of small-scale bombings from the air whose effectiveness has been difficult to ascertain. Far more significant and ominous has been the gradual emasculation of the international community's monitoring and control of Iraq's weapons program.

V

PEACE AND NORMALIZATION

In the mid-1970s, an unusual book was published in Egypt under the title *After the Guns Fall Silent*, written by the Egyptian left-wing intellectual and journalist Muhammad Sid Ahmed.[1] It was the first presentation of an Arab vision of accommodation with Israel, the first Arab effort to spell out what the Middle East might look like after the establishment of Arab-Israeli peace. The author of this bold, pioneering work was roundly criticized in Egypt and elsewhere in the Arab world for breaking a taboo in his endorsing and propagating the idea of peaceful accommodation with Israel. This was so even though the book was written and published after the signing of the Israeli-Egyptian and Israeli-Syrian disengagement agreements, and after two Arab summit conferences had redefined the Arab consensus to embrace the principle of a political settlement with Israel. But a full-fledged vision of Arab-Israeli peace written by a major Egyptian intellectual with left-wing credentials was still difficult for those who remained ideologically and emotionally committed to the struggle against Israel.

In fact, there is a great deal of ambivalence and vacillation at the very core of Sid Ahmed's book. The author began by posing this question: "What shape will the Middle East take after a just and permanent peace?" He then explained that "among Arabs the topic is taboo, condemned as a notion by the bulk of public opinion as well as by most of the intelligentsia. It is condemned because there is a deep-rooted conviction in the Arab psyche that the only conceivable settlement would entail complete surrender." But, he argued, after the October War, which brought more balance to the Israeli-Arab equation, a change occurred in the Arab view of a political settlement. The Arab world decided to settle, "but as long as the settlement with Israel and the future of peace in the region is not embodied in a clearly defined vision, Israel will never admit that the Arab goal is genuine: it will continue to cast doubts on the sincerity of their overtures and maintain that the Arab position is basically unchanged."[2]

It is precisely that "clearly defined vision" that Sid Ahmed set forth. As he saw it, an enduring peace would require Israel to play a "functional role" in the Middle East, comparable to but different from that of Lebanon. "There is . . . more or less tacit acknowledgement that the existence of Israel within secure and recognized borders is unavoidable after the Arabs recover their occupied territories and after the establishment of some Palestinian entity." Then, once settlement is achieved along these lines, the chief psychological barrier to Israel's integration into the region could be addressed: "The stumbling block has

always been the Arabs' fear of Israel's technological superiority and her ability, if peace came to the region, to dom-
inate the Arabs economically and to prevent them from
becoming masters of their own fate."[3]

But Arabs after the October War, buttressed by the use
of the "oil weapon" and having accumulated huge revenues, "acquired a new confidence that Israeli superiority
could no longer deprive them of their freedom of decision—even in the case of peace . . . Israeli quality could
no longer neutralize Arab quantity. . . . For the first time
some kind of match between Israeli technological know-
how and Arab capital can be envisaged in certain quar-
ters." Moreover, in the spirit of "complementarity" there
need be no contradiction between security arrangements
and economic interests. Security arrangements do not
necessarily have to rely on "negative sanctions" (like de-
militarized zones or areas policed by UN forces) but can
actually go hand in hand with "positive incentives" to "promote the interest of the protagonists to abstain from war."

> Industrial projects could conceivably be set up in
> Sinai, in the Negev, the Gaza Strip, the West Bank,
> in various parts of a Palestinian state, and even on
> the borders separating Israel from Syria and South
> Lebanon. Possibly petrochemical plants could be
> erected in some of those regions and more and more
> of the crude oil that now goes to the West could be
> retained to feed these petrochemical complexes. This
> Arab asset could be exported not in the form of crude
> alone but also in the form of finished and semi-
> finished products.[4]

Sid Ahmed saw several advantages in matching security
arrangements with economic-development schemes. Capital could be mobilized for projects that might not be feasible otherwise. Countries like Egypt would benefit by
shifting part of their population from densely populated
regions to desert areas. Advanced industries in an area like
the Sinai could also include "nuclear plants to desalinize
sea water for irrigating wide areas of the desert to meet
growing food requirements." Industrial projects "erected
inside the Palestinian state will invalidate the argument
that this state is not viable."

After a first phase of this kind, during which Israel
would be reluctantly but inevitably absorbed into the life
of the Middle East, a second phase could develop in
which Arabs "could use Israeli human and technological
assets to achieve a Middle East conglomerate able to
stand up to the big geopolitical conglomerates expected to
coalesce at the turn of the century." Curiously, some of Sid
Ahmed's paragraphs read like the vision of Arab-Jewish
co-existence that T. E. Lawrence had sketched out more
than half a century earlier. Most of the time Sid Ahmed
wrote and thought as a Marxist, dialectically—the course
of events being determined by the interplay between
"contradictions." It is thus fully in character that, after
completing the presentation of his impressive ideas about
Arab-Israeli peace, he argued the opposite case: that the
obstacles inherent in the situation are such that implementation is quite unlikely; indeed, that another Arab-
Israeli war may yet be launched.

Most of the "stumbling blocks" the author identified
had to do with Israel itself. Muhammad Sid Ahmed had
come to accept, in fact advocate, the idea of accommoda-

tion with Israel, but he retained a critical, not to say negative, attitude toward the Jewish state, anticipating Israeli

> attempts to break up the settlement into a number of separate agreements . . . in the hope that partial agreements would allow it to neutralize the weaker links instead of dealing with all Arab parties as equals.

But even if a total settlement is achieved, there will be a problem concerning Israel itself. The only justification for its existence is as the embodiment of the Zionist design, and it would lose its *raison d'être* if its role is reduced to that of an economic instrument that the Arab environment would have digested and used for its own development.[5]

Furthermore, "if a settlement is reached, many Arab Jews will eventually return to their original homelands as Israeli emissaries or end up by resettling. Israel has always derived its strength by claiming that its very existence was at stake. Can it continue to obtain foreign aid once this argument loses credibility?" He concluded on a pessimistic note: "For all these reasons Israel will resist being absorbed into the region with all the means at its disposal. That is why a fifth war is likely."[6]

More than twenty years after its publication, *After the Guns Fall Silent* stands out as a unique and exceptionally prescient work in a number of ways. Not merely was it the first work in Arabic to offer and endorse a vision of Arab-Israeli peace, but for many years it remained the only work of its kind. (Not until recently was it supplemented by Hazem Sughria's *In Defense of Peace*.) Sid Ahmed un-

derstood correctly that beyond an agreement enabling Israelis and Arabs to sort out their differences and settle
their conflicts lay complex and difficult questions regarding Israel's own essence, its view of itself, and its role in
the region. For a peace settlement to be durable, Israel
would have to become part of the Middle East and to have
a "function," as he calls it, in its development. For that to
happen, he assumed that Israel would have to undergo a
transformation, and then he posed a legitimate question:
could Israel become an integral part of the Middle East
and retain its own character and cohesion? (Sid Ahmed
held a view common in Egypt that Jews of Middle Eastern
extraction are "Arab Jews" whose ultimate identity has yet
to crystallize.)

Sid Ahmed's ideas regarding the actual cooperation possible between Israel and the Arab states—industrial zones
in border areas, nuclear-powered desalinization plants in
desert areas—are remarkably farsighted. But his ambivalence is as telling: the traces of lingering hostility to Israel,
his doubts, his questions.

Yet the term "peace" has occupied a prominent place in
the vocabulary of Arab-Israeli relations for more than fifty
years. This had not been the case during the early decades
of the Arab-Jewish conflict in and over Palestine, when
the contenders sought victory, accommodation, or political
settlement. The UN partition resolution, the establishment of the state of Israel, the 1948 war, and Israel's victory in it created an entirely different situation. The war
consolidated Israel's existence, but it also expanded and
exacerbated the conflict between the new state and its
Arab surroundings. Yet, in order to normalize its position
and to proceed with its agenda, the new state needed

peace. And peace was for the Arabs to give or deny; this capacity, and the adamant and persistent refusal to extend it, soon became their principal weapon against Israel.

Recent scholarship has shown that Israeli and Arab attitudes toward the notion of a peaceful settlement during the very early stages of the conflict were more complex than had been assumed in subsequent decades, which were characterized by Israeli craving for and Arab rejection of the very idea. During the final phases of the 1948 war and immediately thereafter, several Arab protagonists were willing to discuss peace, but Israeli policy as shaped by David Ben-Gurion preferred armistice agreements to peace treaties. Israel thought the terms demanded by those prospective Arab partners were dangerous, unwarranted, and unacceptable. It preferred to consolidate its existence and preserve its achievements through a more modest series of armistice agreements, and to seek peace later, on a more secure base. Then, during late 1949, when Israel's calculus and policy changed, full-fledged peace agreements proved elusive. King Abdullah of Jordan was the only Arab leader then to conduct—and in fact complete—a peace negotiation with Israel, but when it came to implementation in early 1950, he discovered that he no longer had the authority or the political base for such a bold move.[7]

This brief quest for Arab-Israeli peace was followed by nearly two decades during which peace was an abstract, remote notion. On the Arab side, peace with Israel became equated with capitulation and betrayal. When the president of Tunisia, Habib Bourguiba, proposed in 1965 that the Arab world adopt a "phased strategy"—recognize Israel and continue the struggle through peaceful means—he was denounced as a traitor. Two years later, right after the Six-Day War, the Arab summit conference in Khartoum reiterated and reformulated Arab nationalism's categorical rejection of the very notion of peace with Israel.

On the Israeli side, peace was increasingly considered in mystical terms and as inaccessible, while actual policies focused on meeting Arab political and military challenges. The outcome of the 1967 war altered the situation. The United States shared Israel's view that its victory must be converted into nothing less than a full-fledged peace settlement, and initiated the "territories-for-peace" policy which, through several variations, has guided its conduct to this day. Yet the very idea was initially unacceptable to the defeated Arab states and their supporters and was never accepted by Israel. And, though it informs Security Council Resolution 242, given the UN's need to satisfy diverse and contradictory interests, references to territorial concessions and contractual peace were indirect or coded. Thus peace in the full sense of the term was postponed for another decade, and Middle Eastern diplomacy focused instead on more modest forms of accommodation. When, in February 1971, Egypt's new president, Anwar al-Sadat, communicated through the UN envoy, Gunnar Jarring, his willingness "to enter into a peace agreement with Israel," he probably did not have in mind the full-blown peace treaty he ended up signing in 1979, and Israel did not take his regime and his offer seriously.[8]

Only after the October War was serious thought given to, and work done for, a peaceful resolution of the Arab-Israeli conflict. On the Israeli side, the principal figure was Yitzhak Rabin during his first tenure as prime minister, in

1974–77. (Golda Meir and Moshe Dayan, whose policies collapsed during the war in 1973, saw through the disengagement agreements with Egypt and Syria, but Rabin was left to deal with the long-term consequences.) Rabin's policy was based on two premises: that, at the height of Arab economic power and international political influence, it was not to Israel's advantage to seek a comprehensive settlement; and that Israel could not and should not accept one based on withdrawal to the June 4, 1967, lines. He therefore collaborated with Henry Kissinger in the "step-by-step" diplomacy that led to the September 1975 Israeli-Egyptian interim agreement. On the Arab side, the principle of settling the conflict politically was formally endorsed at the summit conference in Algiers in November 1973. But this meant, as the final communiqué expressed it, acceptance of the Arabs' two premises: that Israel had to withdraw from all Arab territories occupied in June 1967 (including Jerusalem); and that the Palestinians must recover their "established national rights." This was rather vague and could be and indeed was interpreted in more than one way. But Egypt kept edging toward a bolder concept of a peaceful settlement.[9]

Egypt's political and intellectual elite more or less agreed that Egypt must disengage from the policy it had followed vis-à-vis Israel for a quarter-century. Egypt had paid a terrible price for the Six-Day War and the War of Attrition; the oil-producing states of the Gulf had accumulated wealth and influence while Egypt declined. So Cairo's priorities had to be altered. Thus a will to disengage from the conflict with Israel was clear, but it was not matched by a clear sense of how this could or should be achieved. Debates raged. Muhammad Sid Ahmed drew his bold scenario of peace and "complementarity," while others advocated a theory of Israel's "withering" with a more hostile edge: the Arabs would make peace with Israel if the latter withdrew from all territories occupied in June 1967. An Israel "reduced to its natural dimensions," a "second Lebanon," was an entity Egypt and the Arab world could accept; in any event, a shriveled Israel was not viable, would lose coherence and sense of purpose; internal contradictions would come to the fore; and the Israeli state would wither over time.[10] A slightly milder approach was offered by Boutros Boutros-Ghali, then a senior scholar and member of Egypt's foreign-policy establishment:

> In any case, the front-line states may in the near future accept a de jure recognition of Israel, but not the possibility of instituting diplomatic, commercial or cultural relations with it. This is not to say that such relations are inconceivable in the more distant future. It will remain for the State of Israel to prove to the interstate community of the Arab world that it wishes to and is able to integrate itself into the region. This willingness on Israel's part would have to include a vast program of Arabization in which Arabic would become a language of Israel on equal footing with Hebrew[, and] an active process of cultural and social decolonization, in which the policies of both immigration and emigration would be calculated to encourage the integration into the Israeli population only of elements that could adapt to this profound change in the nature of Israeli society. The author does not underestimate the difficulties that would be

created in Israeli society by this sort of change[, but]
only a change of this nature can incur the passage of
the front-line states from a stage of confrontation to
one of coexistence and, from there, to a level of active cooperation without which there can be no real
or durable peace in the area.[11]

The debate ended with the direct Egyptian-Israeli negotiation predicated on the principle of "land for peace."
The bilateral part of the Camp David Accords and the
subsequent peace treaty rested on a clear formula: Israel's
full withdrawal from the Sinai Peninsula in return for contractual peace, "normalized" relations, and a satisfactory
security regime. But the same clarity did not apply to the
"framework for peace." Disagreements over the implementation of the "autonomy plan" for Palestinians marred
the new relationship, and the initial hopes that Israel's relations with the Arab world would be transformed were
dashed.

Before this turn of events, Israelis had time to think seriously about the meaning of peace. It was no longer an
abstract notion wrapped in mist but a concrete, accessi-
ble goal. Egypt was opened to Israeli tourists in 1979
and thousands traveled to Cairo, Alexandria, and Upper
Egypt. Israelis were engaged in drawing up bold plans as
well as in soul-searching. When borders were open and
people could move in both directions, would Israel lose
its coherence and identity? Would Israeli Jews of Middle
Eastern extraction perhaps feel more comfortable in
Egypt than in Israel's Westernized culture?[12]

But by 1981 it had become clear that the "framework
for peace" was doomed. The "cold peace" meant that

diplomatic relations and some elements of "normal relations" were implemented and maintained, that the security regime in the Sinai was adhered to, but a critical, negative tone came to characterize Cairo's attitude and policy toward Israel.

This selective policy enabled Egypt to maintain the basic, most important elements of its new relationship with Israel and to cultivate its new relationship with the United States while at the same time placating Islamist and leftist opposition and mending fences in the Arab world. But some Israelis criticized and complained: this was not the peace they had yearned for and envisioned. Among other Israelis, who had felt uncomfortable with the prospects of opening up to the Arab world, of losing the comfort of a familiar way of life, there was a lack of genuine interest in Arab social and cultural life. (It is significant that no correspondent for an Israeli newspaper or television station has been stationed over time in Cairo.) In January 1999, Ariel Sharon, addressing a closed session of Israeli diplomats in New York, expressed the atavistic discomfort most Israelis seem to have with the prospect of open borders between Israel and her Arab neighbors: "If we keep open borders—which may be a vision of this peace [process]—Israel would be swamped by many vehicles, would become a country of transit; hundreds of thousands of Arab visitors would come carrying not swords in their hands but olive leaves in their mouths . . . this is a very complex issue that will have to be thought through."[13]

This Israeli frame of mind might conceivably have been altered, with the gradual development of new ties, but that was not allowed to happen. Instead, both sides settled into the new reality of a limited selective relationship.

Thousands of Israelis went to Egypt as tourists; very few Egyptians came to Israel. Curiously, an Israeli Academic Center was allowed to open in Cairo, but it was rendered controversial by the unruly media, and its effect was in any event limited because it was boycotted by Egypt's hostile intelligentsia and academic establishment.

The Israeli assumption that peace with the largest, most important, and most powerful Arab state would go a long way toward ending the Arab-Israeli conflict proved wrong. That Egypt had made a full peace with Israel had no profound immediate effect elsewhere in the Arab world. The termination of the military conflict between Egypt and Israel tended to telescope rather than limit the Arab-Israeli conflict. Indeed, resolution of the Israeli-Egyptian conflict only exacerbated the Palestinian, Syrian, and Lebanese dimensions of Israel's situation. Hardly less damaging was the realization that peace could be made and maintained without a genuine reconciliation. Menachem Begin had wanted a separate peace with Egypt, and at this he proved to be quite successful, but it fell short of being the peace Israelis yearned for.

The lengthy suspension of the peace process finally ended with the Madrid Conference in October 1991 and its new concept of four tracks of bilateral negotiations (with Israel's immediate neighbors: Syria, Lebanon, Jordan, and the Palestinians) and a parallel track of multilateral negotiations. As we have seen, the multilateral efforts were made by five working groups concerned with refugees, water, arms control and regional security, environmental problems, and economic development. Arab states from the Gulf and North Africa and interested states from other parts of the world were invited to join these working groups. By dealing with issues that were meant to be solved after the resolution of Israeli-Arab political disputes, the parties could glimpse the prospect of regional cooperation, and this in turn could facilitate the difficult bilateral negotiations. This proved to be a particularly productive idea. The multilateral talks were successful both in their own right and as a launch for the regional economic conferences that were the high-water mark of the peace process in the mid-1990s.

It was through these multilateral talks that a nation like Saudi Arabia came to participate in the peace process. The Saudis had been sharply critical of Sadat's original peace-making with Israel, but time had changed their perspective and priorities. The Iranian revolution of 1979, the rise of a powerful Iraqi state, and the tidal wave of radical Islam all over the Middle East presented new and ominous threats to the kingdom's survival and prosperity. In the perspective afforded by these developments, the Israeli challenge lost much of its edge. In fact, Egyptian-Israeli peace and stabilization at the core of the Middle East came to be seen as a positive development, for it would help contain Iran, Iraq, and the radical tide in the Gulf. The signing of the Oslo Accords legitimized a significant measure of Saudi-Israeli normalization. It was a first step, still a far cry from the Arab definition of a "just peace," but if "the sole legitimate representative" of Palestinian nationalism had crossed the threshold and agreed to mutual recognition with Israel, why should Saudis, Omanis, and Tunisians refuse to discuss future regional projects with Israelis in a multilateral working group?

Rabin approached all these new developments in his

customary pragmatic way. Israel faced both an opportunity and a duty. The availability of the Madrid framework, the evident changes in Arab attitudes, the hospitable regional and international arenas all offered unusual chances to move the peace process forward, and it was Israel's duty to take advantage of them. But it was not at all clear how far and along which course the peace process could be moved. As Rabin saw it, Israel should indicate its willingness, explore the options, make progress where progress could be made, and make fresh decisions along the way.

Rabin's approach was incrementalist. As he had in the mid-1970s, he shied away from a sweeping approach to a comprehensive or swift settlement. A final resolution was not feasible, and whatever version of it was available came with a prohibitively high cost. Israel's first step should be made with either the Palestinians or the Syrians, and the next step should depend on that first breakthrough and be tailored to the circumstances. And so it was that the first agreement was with the PLO and that it was followed by peace with Jordan. Rabin was surprised by the willingness of other Arab states to normalize relations with Israel and to participate in the regional economic conferences in Casablanca and Amman. But with no agreement with Syria, the road to a formal resolution of the Arab-Israeli conflict was closed. Still, Rabin was not in a hurry. Much had been accomplished in only a few years, and the difficult job of completing the final-status negotiations with the Palestinians and the arduous negotiation with Syria would have to be carried out during a second term.

Peres, as we have seen, approached the peace process in an entirely different way. He was mindful of all the difficult political and territorial disputes between Israel and its Arab neighbors, but to him these were not the crucial matter. They would be addressed in the first, transitional phase, during which trust and confidence should build, but "in the second, decisive phase of the peace process the specific nature of peace is the dominant issue."[14] And its nature would be determined by the interplay between Arab-Israeli relations and the larger regional developments of which they were a part. In short, a durable solution to the Arab-Israeli problem could be achieved only when the Middle East had established a regional system, and the formation of such a system depended on the resolution of the Arab-Israeli conflict. Put differently, Israel could not enjoy a stable peace so long as the Middle East was beset by severe social and economic problems, and Israel's neighbors could not overcome their problems so long as they failed to settle their conflict with Israel. The foreign minister's vision was stated boldly:

Peace between Israel and its Arab neighbors will create the environment for a basic reorganization of Middle Eastern institutions. Reconciliation and Arab acceptance of Israel as a nation with equal rights and responsibilities will sire a new sort of cooperation—not only between Israel and its neighbors but also among Arab nations. It will change the face of the region and its ideological climate. . . .

The problems of this region of the world cannot be solved by individual nations. . . . Regional organization is the key to peace and security. . . . Our ultimate goal is the creation of a regional community of nations . . . modeled on the European community.[15]

As Rabin's foreign minister and partner, Peres was given considerable scope to try to implement some of his ideas. He helped initiate the "donors' conference" in Washington, two weeks after the signing ceremony on the White House lawn; this was intended to orchestrate a large-scale international boost to the Palestinian economy and to raise living standards in the Gaza Strip and the West Bank. Indeed, the point was to recast the economic relationship between Israel and the West Bank and the Gaza Strip (the legal framework having been defined in the Paris Agreement in July 1994). This campaign was motivated by more than the obvious and familiar idea that Arab peace-makers should be rewarded economically. As American and Israeli policy-makers saw it, Hamas and the other fundamentalist groups who opposed Arafat fed on poverty; by creating new sources of employment, by providing housing projects and better schools, the Palestinian Authority could better build a constituency that supported peace with Israel. A different way of saying much the same thing was to say that over time it would be hard if not impossible to maintain peace between a society enjoying a per capita income of $18,000 a year and a society with a per capita income of less than $1,000 a year. That is difficult enough between neighboring states separated by clearly defined boundaries, and even more so in the case of two societies whose lives are closely intertwined.

Israel's efforts to get financial and economic aid to the Palestinian Authority was a controversial aspect of the Rabin-Peres policy—controversial in Israel and among Jewish communities abroad. After years of mobilizing *against* Arafat and the PLO, it was difficult to accept the reconciliation, the recognition, the symbolism of a hand-shake, and even harder to imagine Israeli leaders and diplomats lobbying to obtain financial resources for yesterday's enemies. Yet this went to the core of the new reality that Israeli policy-makers were seeking to shape. Israelis have yet to decide whether they want a clear-cut separation from the Palestinians or some form of association or integration. But whatever shape the final settlement takes, the very existence of the Oslo Accords means that it has ceased to be a zero-sum game. Mental adjustment to this revolutionary truth has lagged far behind, for understandable reasons. The Rabin government, and Foreign Minister Peres in particular, were way ahead of the public in adjusting to this new reality and molding it to fit into a new policy about Israel and its Arab environment.

Under Peres's direction, then, experts affiliated with the Foreign Ministry prepared an impressive dossier of joint economic projects. Of particular significance were the industrial parks proposed for several sites along the lines separating Israel from the West Bank and the Gaza Strip, to be financed by international agencies and private investors, and intended to provide employment for Palestinian workers while facilitating Israeli-Palestinian economic cooperation and minimizing friction or the appearance of Israeli economic domination. (The similarity to some of the ideas raised nearly twenty years earlier by Muhammad Sid Ahmed is quite striking.) In short order, a similar approach was likely for Israel's relationship with Jordan. King Hussein made clear that he expected "peace dividends"—debt relief and military aid from the United States and massive investments in Jordan's economy that would make up for the loss of remittances from Jordanian workers in the Gulf. He also indicated that he was willing to develop a "warm peace" with Israel, in stark contrast to Egypt's proverbial "cold" policy. The Foreign Ministry responded with a thick volume of projects focused on the Jordan rift valley. It included spectacular infrastructure projects (for example, a canal leading from the Dead Sea to a single Red Sea port just above the Gulf of Eilat, and a joint international airport for Eilat and Aqaba) as well as more conventional industrial parks in border areas.

It was during Peres's secret visit with King Hussein in November 1993 that an international business conference was first proposed. (Peres wanted to hold it in Amman.) The Israeli effort to take advantage of the Oslo Accords so as finally to make peace with Jordan had just begun, and Peres was seeking to expand the agenda. In the winter of 1993–94, the king was not quite ready for such a bold move, but the Clinton administration was persuaded to endorse the idea and helped to recruit Morocco's King Hassan: the first conference took place in Casablanca a year later, the second one in Amman in November 1995. Both conferences were impressive and successful gatherings of many Israeli, Arab, and international businessmen, though it is difficult to point out many joint Arab-Israeli business ventures that grew out of them; still, as a demonstration of the potentials inherent in the peace process, they were most effective. So Peres pushed on and tried to put together a regional bank for the Middle East, modeled after regional banks in other parts of the world. He came quite close to seeing this project through, but neither the Clinton administration nor most Arab states had been fully supportive of this concept, and with the waning of the peace process it was shelved *sine die*.

The differences between Rabin's and Peres's approaches to peace-making were underlined by the
changes Peres introduced when he assumed power in November 1995, after Rabin's assassination, in the conduct of
Israel's negotiation with Syria. Rabin had assumed that Israel could not expect to obtain more than a "cold" peace
with Syria, tailored by Assad to offer less than Sadat had
given. A warmer, closer relationship could develop only
over time. But a contractual peace and satisfactory security regime would remove the danger of conventional war,
push Iran back to the margins of the Middle East, resolve
Israel's problem in Lebanon, and consolidate the agreements with Jordan and the Palestinians. These achievements would justify the concessions Israel would have to
offer Damascus.

Peres was not interested in yet another version of
Egypt's "cold peace," and thought it would be difficult to
persuade the Israeli public to withdraw from the Golan
Heights in return. But if Syria's economy could be tied
more closely to the global economy, if investments were
brought to it, if joint Israeli-Syrian ventures could be
launched (even, if necessary, with American sponsorship
or partnership), a web of interests would develop that
would reduce the danger of renewed conflict. And if some
of these joint ventures were established in the Golan
Heights, this cordon would be hardly less valuable as security protection than yet another line of fortifications.
And Syria would have to think twice before embarking on
a course that would jeopardize its investments and interests in the Golan. Joint ventures in the Golan would also
make Israeli concessions easier, blunting the sense of loss

and departure. In the terminology of conflict-resolution theory—whereas Rabin was seeking a "settlement" with Syria, Peres was aiming at a "resolution."

Further, Peres wanted to make a prospective agreement with Syria a stepping stone to a comprehensive Arab-Israeli settlement. In his discussions with the Clinton administration he explored the idea of a regional-security system in the Middle East, though the Americans regarded it as premature. Meanwhile, discussions between Israel and Turkey matured to produce a formal agreement on strategic cooperation. In theory, this Turkish-Israeli relationship could fit into a regional system inclusive of the major Arab states, but in practice Israel's Arab interlocutors, first and foremost Syria, viewed it as an anti-Arab measure, a revival of David Ben-Gurion's "alliance of the periphery" in the late 1950s.

Nor was Assad enamored of the economic aspects of Peres's peace policy, which he had already denounced as an Israeli scheme directed against Arab nationalism. He found the notion of joint businesses an offensive intrusion: any Israeli involvement in projects in the Golan Heights would be interpreted as perpetuating its presence there and denying him the chance for a full liberation of Syrian territories lost in 1967. As Assad's biographer, Patrick Seale, put it: "Most Syrians would have seen such a settlement as exposing their society, nascent industries, cultural traditions and national security to hostile Israeli penetration. For Asad it would have made a mockery of his entire career."[16]

It is telling that negotiations between Israel and Syria collapsed in March 1996 for reasons that had little to do with this dim view of economic relations with Israel in the event of peace and more to do with Assad's response to the initiative of an Israeli prime minister who was eager to come to an agreement with him. Assad had negotiated with Israel resentfully and grudgingly because it was something he had been forced to do, and now his policy options had diminished. As a grudging peace-maker, he would agree only to what he could not avoid, and he would demonstrate his dissatisfaction with the way things were going. Assad at one and the same time criticized everyone who deviated from the course he had tried to prescribe—who, in his view, gave Israel too much and undermined him—and was criticized by Syrians and others adamantly opposed to peace with Israel, who expected or wanted him to uphold the ideas and principles they had once been identified with. For those who thought and said that terms like "revolution," "Arab unity," and "Arab socialism" had long ago lost their meaning, that the Ba'ath had become a hollow term, but who were hoping against hope that Assad would hold the line, his willingness to sign a contractual peace with Israel was a bitter disappointment.

The lines separating Assad's position from that of his critics and from that of the objects of his own criticism are landmarks, and when we try to map out—and understand—Arab attitudes to peace-making with Israel, we must understand where they are. Each end of the spectrum is clear and distinct: the wholehearted opposition of Islamic and other ideological opponents to any peace or reconciliation, and open and unambiguous advocacy of full peace with Israel. In the middle of the spectrum, sub-

tle differences separate halfhearted endorsement of reconciliation from a grudging reluctance to agree to peace
and from criticism of all agreements with Israel.

"Orphaned peace" is the term Fouad Ajami uses to de-
scribe a diplomacy that Arab opinion has accepted with
many reservations.[17] Popular opinion in any country is difficult to measure, and especially in Arab countries, but
there seems to be no discrepancy in this case between
popular opinion and the positions articulated by public intellectuals and the intelligentsia. They are all informed
with a sense of defeat. These have not been good years in
the Arab world. Old ideologies have died or become stale
and have not been replaced; the great hopes of the "oil
decade" have long ago been dashed. Saddam Hussein was
defeated in the Gulf War, and though his immediate
neighbors were relieved, there were those who had hoped
for a revival of revolutionary zeal, spirit, and ideals, and
they have been badly disappointed. The end of the Cold
War and the disintegration of the Soviet Union left the
United States with undue influence in the Middle East.
Political Islam, a source both of threat and regeneration,
seemed to have peaked. And even if the Arab regimes are
remarkably resilient, durability does not go hand in hand
with openness and innovation. Against that backdrop,
peace with Israel achieved on terms closer to the Israeli
than to the Arab position was received as yet another humiliation.

The expatriate Syrian poet Nizar Qabbani, one of the
most eloquent and bitter critics of the "Arab order," wrote
a particularly powerful and poignant poem, published in
October 1995, expressing his disgust with the Oslo Ac-

cords and with the "Arab condition" exposed by them. "The last walls of embarrassment have fallen," he wrote; "we were delighted and we danced and we blessed ourselves for signing the peace of the cowards."[18] This was a humiliating surrender, with Arabs scrambling to kiss the shoes of "the killer. . . . In our hands they left a sardine can called Gaza and a dry bone called Jericho. . . . After the secret romance in Oslo, we came out barren. They gave us a homeland smaller than a single grain of wheat." And it was a deal made in the United States—"the dowry was in dollars . . . the cake was a gift from America." But Qabbani's real rage was directed at the Arabs' own political establishment, whom he held responsible for the misery and humiliation in the terms of the peace with Israel and for the larger decline of which the Oslo Accords were both a consequence and a symptom:

> *Who would ask the rulers*
> *about the peace of cowards*
> *about the peace of selling in installments*
> *and renting in installments*
> *about the peace of the merchants*
> *and the exploiters?*
> *Who could ask them*
> *about the peace of the dead?*
> *They have silenced the street*
> *and murdered all the questions*
> *and those who question.*

What Qabbani said in verse, others said in prose. The most prominent Palestinian intellectual, Edward Said, who had been one of Arafat's supporters several years earlier, denounced the Oslo Accords as a "sell-out." In *The Politics of Dispossession*, he wrote:

> With some of the euphoria dissipated after the great celebration surrounding the breakthrough, it now becomes possible to reexamine the Israeli-PLO agreements with the required common sense. What emerges from such scrutiny is a deal that is more flawed and weighted unfavorably for the Palestinian people than many had first supposed. The show biz front of the White House ceremony on September 13, the degrading spectacle of Yasir Arafat thanking everyone for the suspension of most of his people's rights and the solemnity of Bill Clinton's performance . . . all these only temporarily obscure the truly astonishing proportions of the quite sudden Palestinian capitulation, which smacks of the PLO leadership's exhaustion and of Israel's shrewdness. . . .
>
> In sum, we need to move up from a state of supine abjectness with which, in reality, the Oslo DoP was negotiated . . . into the prosecution of parallel agreements with Israel and the Arabs that concern Palestinian national, as opposed to municipal aspirations. But this does not exclude resistance against the Israeli occupation, which continues indefinitely.[19]

Qabbani's poem was entitled "Al-Muharwilun" ("The Hurried Ones")—a castigating term for the Arabs who rushed to normalize relations with Israel. This term, used by an angry poet to denounce the Arab governments for endorsing hated agreements, diplomacy, and policies—the Egyptian and Syrian governments, notably—was the very term Arab governments themselves used to criticize those whom they accused of eagerness to "normalize" relations with Israel too rapidly. This underlines two important aspects of the Arab attitude to peace-making with Israel: the centrality of the notion of "normalization," and the complex relationship between the ruling political classes and their societies on this particular issue. As Ajami has correctly pointed out, reservations with regard to peace-making with Israel were one issue on which autocratic governments and their "civil societies" could agree, and in which they could have agreed on a division of labor, as it were. If it suited Sadat and Mubarak to keep the peace with Israel "cold," they might as well also let Egyptian professional associations boycott their Israeli counterparts, or let the Egyptian press vent their anger and frustration in anti-Israeli diatribes. By the same token, for a Syrian regime that was negotiating a peace with Israel and trying to achieve its extremely narrow concept of peace, statements made by Syrian writers or journalists condemning "normalization with Israel" would be useful. Nor could Arafat complain of Edward Said, Hisham Sharabi, or other prominent Palestinian intellectuals for criticizing the Oslo process when he himself publicly indicated that "the struggle continues."

During the mid-1990s, the term "normalization" came to replace "cold peace" as the key term in discussing the nature of Arab-Israeli peace. Curiously and significantly, this focused the debate on a notion that had been so cardinal to the original purpose of Zionism, which sought to normalize the condition of the Jews by establishing a state in which the Jewish people could develop a normal society and a normal economy. As we saw, this failed to happen in

1949. A Jewish state was founded and survived the 1948
war, but it could not obtain the Arab states' acceptance of
its very existence. The most effective weapons in the
Arabs' conflict with the Jewish state were refusal, rejection,
and boycott. So the new state was rejected by its immediate neighbors, by the Muslim world, later by the Soviet
bloc and much of the Third World. Israel did very well
nonetheless, but its regional and international positions
were not normal. Peace with the Arabs was the key to normalizing both. The end of the Cold War and the inauguration of the Madrid process improved Israel's international
position, but normalizing "the Israeli condition" could not
be achieved without resolution of the Arab-Israeli conflict.

As new agreements were being negotiated, signed, and
implemented in the years 1992–95, "normalization" acquired two different meanings: the establishment of bilateral "normal peaceful relations" between Israel and each
of its principal Arab counterparts; and the further normalization of Israel's position in the Middle East through its
participation in regional and international forums along
with Arab and other partners. The Arabs' response to Israel's quest for normalization varied greatly. Syria's original
position in the bilateral negotiations of 1992–93 was that
"normalization" fell outside the scope of the "peace" legitimized by the Arab consensus for regaining the territories
Syria had lost in 1967. The Syrians grudgingly accepted
the notion of a contractual peace, but continued to argue
that the Israeli definition of normality—in cultural, com-
mercial, and economic relations, for instance—concerned
issues that "the society" and not the government should
agree to, and that conditions allowing for such relations
could develop only over time. In August 1993, when Ra-

bin made his "hypothetical gambit" and included "normalization" in Israel's peace proposal, Assad responded by
telling Warren Christopher that he "disliked" and "had
difficulties" with that term; it took Syria another year of
trilateral negotiations with Israel and the United States to
agree to a limited, well-defined "normalization" as part of
its prospective peaceful relationship with Israel. This Syrian attitude clearly reflected the Assad regime's negotiating style. All issues and details were a matter of hard
bargaining: the more eager Israel was for normalization,
the higher the price it would have to pay for it.

Also, Syria was understandably trying to follow the
Egyptian precedent of "cold peace." Egypt had signed a
full-fledged peace treaty, with numerous annexes concerning normalization across the board, and it had subsequently found a way to turn these agreements into a dead
letter while keeping the essence and formality of a non-
belligerent relationship. Perhaps Syria could accomplish
the same result by avoiding the "normalization" issue al-
together. Moreover, Assad felt he must do better than
merely replicate Egypt's agreement with Israel (if his
agreement with Israel looked like a copy of the Camp
David Accords, he would be hard put to explain why he
had not made it fifteen years earlier) and tried to achieve
something that at least in one major aspect would seem
better than the peace made by Sadat. In time, Assad discovered that he could not cite the precedent Egypt had
set in obtaining full withdrawal of Israeli troops from its
territory without offering an equivalent full contractual
"peace with normalization," at least on paper.

Beyond these considerations lay genuine fears of Israel's
ambitions and schemes in the event of peace. Assad was

not about to open Syria up to Israeli business and technology, or to contemplate the creation of a "new Middle East" on the ruins of what was after all a predominantly Arab world. The thesis has been advanced that Assad is so deeply concerned with the destabilizing effects of peace with Israel that he does not actually want to consummate the deal and conducts negotiations in an "idle" mode.[20] But this is an overstatement. Assad believes that his regime can cope with the effects of peace and limited normalization with Israel, but his aim is to contain Israel, not to integrate it into the Middle East. In October 1995, he lashed out against the very idea:

> I wonder about this notion in the far Arab future and what its values and role at present and in the future will be. . . .
> This is the objective they are seeking. . . . Why is the Middle East being established? The Middle East already exists. The strange thing is that the Middle East is being presented as an alternative to Arabism. . . .[21]

As I have tried to make clear, Assad in 1995 was locked in an awkward position vis-à-vis the Israeli architect of an envisioned "new Middle East" who was willing to move much further than Rabin had been, but who insisted on "quality" and "depth" in the new peaceful relationship, and who saw normalization and economic cooperation as key to it. Assad's difficulties with this very approach were an important element in the subsequent failure to achieve a breakthrough.

As for Egypt, though there is a domestic dimension to its

negativism about normalization with Israel,[22] the accent is clearly on the regional dimension. Egypt shared Syria's anxieties about a "new Middle East," but whereas Damascus voiced opposition and criticism from the sidelines, Cairo was forced, by virtue of being both a pillar of the peace process and a critic of its excesses, to adopt a much more complex policy. Its dilemmas were simplified by Netanyahu's victory and by the subsequent decline of peace diplomacy, for Israel's regional role diminished and Cairo could shift from subtle, indirect criticism of overly eager, hurried, and premature Arab willingness to normalize relations with Israel to outright criticism of normalization as such. "Normalization is an Israeli invention," stated Osama al-Baz, a particularly thoughtful Egyptian policy-maker, "which means the establishment of a special relationship. Such a relationship must be predicated on a common concept of and common interests in the future, and these are absent of true progress and of a national, normal Israeli conduct, which meets legal criteria; normal relations cannot be maintained lest the balance be upset."[23]

Jordan formulated its peace policy in yet a third way. It was willing to offer Israel a distinctly "warm" peace in return for rewards it expected to gain from other dimensions of its relationship with its neighbor. The Hashemite regime had no qualms about the effect of normalized relations with Israel in its own domestic sphere or about Israel's playing a regional role at the expense of some of Jordan's rivals. But the course of events in recent years has made this policy untenable. Rabin's assassination, public resistance at home, the failure of the anticipated "peace dividends" to materialize, and the general decline of peace diplomacy forced King Hussein to turn down the volume

on peace and normalization. And now Israel's relationship
with Jordan does not appear very different from its relationship with Egypt.

At the same time, the Palestinian approach is remarkably uninhibited. This may sound surprising, given the fe-
rocity of the Israeli-Palestinian conflict, but it is quite
understandable when the realities of two societies intertwined with one another are taken into account. In any
event, the Palestinians' leverage in the peace process de-
rives primarily from their centrality in determining the legitimacy and finality of a settlement. This crucial issue
goes to the core of Israel's relationship with the Arab
world. Israel appears to Arabs as a powerful, aggressive,
and threatening entity, but in fact it is a country haunted
by a sense of vulnerability and persecution. Arabs believe
as a rule that time is on their side, and many Israelis agree.
But they have different views of a final settlement as a result. As Israelis see it, they are offering, irreversibly, to
give up tangible assets, and they would like to be reassured that the consequent settlement is definitive and final, not open-ended. This is matched by a tendency on the
Arabs' side to deny Israel that very asset—a reassuring
sense of finality.

Since the Cairo conference in June 1996, there has
been an official Arab definition of the terms under which
a comprehensive Arab-Israeli peace might be established
(and, implicitly, the Arab-Israeli conflict might end):

Adhering to their national responsibility, the Arab
leaders assert that the establishment of a comprehensive and just peace in the Middle East requires
Israel's complete withdrawal from all occupied Pales-

tinian territories, including Arab Jerusalem, and enabling the Palestinian people to exercise their right to
self-determination and to establish an independent
state with Arab Jerusalem as its capital. This is because the Palestinian issue is the crux of the Arab-
Israeli conflict. The Arab leaders also call for Israel's
complete withdrawal from the Syrian Golan Heights
to the June 4, 1967, line and for Israel's full and un-
conditional withdrawal from southern Lebanon and
the western al-Biqa to the internationally recognized
borders, in implementation of Security Council Resolutions 242, 338, and 425 and the principle of land for
peace. On these bases, they call for the resumption of
talks on all tracks.

The Arab countries' commitment to continue the
peace process to achieve a just and comprehensive
peace under the aegis of international legitimacy is
a goal and a strategic option. This commitment requires similar serious and unequivocal commitment
on the part of Israel, which must work to complete
the peace process in a way that will restore the rights
and occupied territories and ensure balanced and
equal security for all the states of the region, in accordance with the principles agreed upon at the
Madrid Conference, especially the land-for-peace
principles, and the assurances given to the parties.

The Arab leaders stress their adherence to the UN
resolutions, which do not accept or recognize any situation resulting from Israeli settlement activity in the
occupied Arab territories. They consider this settlement activity illegal, unlawful, and nonbinding. They
consider the building of settlements and bringing set-

tlers to them a violation of the Geneva Convention and the Madrid framework and an obstruction of the peace process. They call for a halt to all settlement activity in the occupied Syrian Golan Heights and the occupied Palestinian territories, particularly Jerusalem, and for the dismantling of these settlements. They also reject any change to the character and legal status of Arab Jerusalem. They emphasize that a comprehensive and just peace in the Middle East cannot be achieved unless a solution is found for the issue of Jerusalem and for the problem of *Palestinian refugees*, who *have the right to return* in accordance with international legitimacy and the UN resolutions.[24] [Italics mine.]

By citing the Palestinian "right of return" as yet another condition, the Arabs introduced an element likely to perpetuate indefinitely the debate on a settlement. It is hard enough to formulate a definition of terms for a final settlement that will be acceptable to a large and diverse group, and within that group particularly important parts are played by the Palestinians and by Egypt. The "right of return" is an important issue of principle particularly for Palestinians living in the diaspora, but it is significant first and foremost as an issue likely to keep the peace process open-ended.

Egypt has been quite open and systematic in formulating a policy designed to achieve the same end. That policy was expounded in detail by President Mubarak in May 1998 at a forum of the French Institute for International Relations in Paris. "You may agree with me," he said (according to the unpublished minutes), "that the implementation of peace in the Middle East, as in other regions, requires elements that I will call indispensable elements, around which a national consensus can form particularly among the active sectors of the society." He then enumerated nine, beginning with "a popular perception that the proposed peace formula is a just formula that accomplished the required balance between the rights and commitments of the two parties. In the absence of such justice peace rests on a fragile base and will be blown by the first gust of wind. . . ." A stable peace, he went on, had to be based on international legitimacy, free will of and acceptance by the parties, comprehensiveness, and balanced security. As could be expected, he also said that Israel should give up its "military nuclear program" and sign the Nuclear Non-Proliferation Treaty.

Yet Egyptian policy on Israel has always had many strands. While formulating an open-ended definition of peace and pursuing a policy of cold peace, of opposition to "normalization," and of open enmity to Netanyahu's government, Mubarak's regime has also given a significant number of Egyptian intellectuals the green light to join a regional peace movement together with Israelis, Jordanians, and Palestinians. The group met for the first time in Copenhagen in February 1997 and has met several times since. Egyptian opponents of the peace process vehemently criticized the Egyptian participants, but Israelis were rightly impressed more by their willingness to articulate a public defense of peace with Israel than by these familiar denunciations.

In this present phase of Arab-Israeli relations, there is no Arab consensus or dominant view with regard to peace with Israel. But in the gamut of Arab views, those of

Egypt and of the Palestinians are notable. Egypt is, after all, the senior Arab state, and the Palestinians are the "core of the problem." Yet Arafat, the PLO, and the Palestinian Authority are not the sole spokesmen for the Palestinian cause. By signing the Oslo Accords and by administering an actual government with authority over land and people, Arafat and his organization became part of the established order. Political opponents and public intellectuals can articulate a Palestinian position free from the moderating effects of power and responsibility. It is interesting that two different Palestinian intellectuals operating in entirely different contexts have recently argued for a "bi-national state" as the preferred solution to the Israeli-Palestinian conflict.

Edward Said, whose break with Arafat and criticism of the Oslo Accords I have already mentioned, wrote a brief essay published on January 10, 1999, in *The New York Times Magazine* in which he argued that neither Israel's policy of separation nor the Palestinians' quest for independent statehood could work: "For all this, the problem is that Palestinian self-determination in a separate state is unworkable, just as unworkable as the principle of separation between a demographically mixed, irreversibly connected Arab population without sovereignty and a Jewish population with it. The question, I believe, is not how to devise means for persisting in trying to separate them but to see whether it is possible for them to live together as fairly and peacefully as possible."

Dr. Azmi Bishara, a member of the Knesset and an eloquent spokesman, in excellent Hebrew, for Israel's Arab citizens, in 1998 gave a lengthy interview to an Israeli magazine in which, among other things, he stated:

I do not rule out a temporary solution of two states
for two peoples, but this cannot be more than a temporary solution . . . ultimately the framework must be
bi-national. . . .

A distinction must be made between a historic
compromise and a settlement. A settlement can be
made without a historic compromise, but it would be
limited in its time range and would lack the moral
and historic dimensions. . . . [The Zionist left] speaks
about the '67 problem as if the '48 problem did not
exist. . . . If you ask me whether a Zionist peace is
possible I would say that a settlement, maybe even a
comparatively just settlement, is possible but not final, comprehensive peace, the end of the conflict. In
such an event the struggle against Zionism will continue in other forms. It could possibly turn from a
national to a civic struggle. In that case our role as
Arab citizens of Israel could become the most important. . . .

If we speak of the national conflict the solution is
the decolonization of the occupied territories in the
West Bank and Gaza. But if we speak of the civic
problem the solution is Israel's dezionization.

These various notions of peace among Israel's Arab
partners do not mesh well with Israel's own biases and
preferences. Israelis are preoccupied in this context with
two principal issues: (1) the quality, or depth, of peace,
and (2) the finality of the political settlement. As we have
seen, there is widespread opposition in the Arab world to
the very idea of normalization as such, but Israelis regard
Arab willingness to offer it or refusal to do so as an impor-

tant criterion for measuring the value, stability, and durability of an agreement.

Israelis attribute an even greater significance to the
Arabs' attachment to open-ended formulations, and to
other expressions of their reluctance to accept a definitive
resolution of the conflict, all of which inflame the Israelis'
underlying sense of insecurity. Whether it is the Egyptian
practice of changing the definition of "satisfactory settlement" or the vows taken by radical Palestinian intellectuals and political activists never to accept the legitimacy of
Zionism, the impact on the public and political debate in
Israel is negative. Clearly better to have cold peace rather
than hot war with Egypt, but the kind of peace Egypt
offers reduces the Israeli motivation to leave the Golan Heights in return for a peace agreement with Syria
when that agreement is likely to fall short of the familiar
Egyptian-Israeli model.

The Palestinians, a weaker protagonist, do not project
the same potential threat that Egypt does, should its current relationship with Israel sour. But their special status
endows their acceptance or rejection of a settlement with
unique significance. Yasser Arafat is aware of this and has
been determined to use it as an asset at his disposal. But
even if Arafat abandons all ambiguity as part of a final settlement, Palestinian intellectuals and ideologues are likely
to hoist the banner that today is carried by Said, Bishara,
and others, and to argue that the settlement is unjust, that
the conflict is not over, that the struggle must continue.
The power they would be wielding would be that of ideas
and emotions, no more, no less.

VI

THE NEW AGENDA

As early 1999 has shown, the short-term agenda of the Israeli-Arab peace process is shaped primarily, and yet again, by Israeli elections; the focal point is May 17, 1999. A few months earlier, the focal point seemed to be May 4, 1999—the expiration date of the five-year transitional period established by the Oslo Accords, which raised the prospect of a unilateral declaration of Palestinian independence and statehood. That issue was addressed at the Wye River Conference; an undertaking by Arafat to abstain from making such a declaration was apparently an unpublicized part of the deal. Then, when Netanyahu's government fell, early elections were announced in Israel, and implementation of the Wye Agreement was suspended, Arafat nonetheless persisted in his resolve to postpone his decision. Arafat and his associates estimated, correctly, that a declaration of Palestinian statehood on May 4 would play into Netanyahu's hands on May 17. Also, restraint in this matter was part of their strategy to build a new relationship with Washington, and they were willing to sacrifice some other gains and assets for this larger purpose. Moreover, it was not at all certain that a unilateral declaration of independence and statehood would prove to be a clear achievement.

Like the 1996 election, the general elections of 1999 have been cast as a referendum on Israel's relationship with the Arab world and on the peace process. This in itself was a success for Prime Minister Netanyahu, who realized that he would be vulnerable in a campaign focused on his personality, his social policies, or his government's performance. Netanyahu used his position as prime minister and his skills as a political tactician, campaigner, and communicator to present himself as the leader who could provide both peace and security, who knew how to stand up to the Arabs, who could avoid or minimize concessions, and who could get a better deal in the forthcoming final-status negotiations and in the other tests awaiting Israel.

This was, of course, quite incongruous with the substance of the Wye Agreement and with the rationale that Netanyahu and Sharon offered just a few months earlier when signing it. The discrepancy was pointed out by Netanyahu's rivals on his right (Benny Begin and Herut) and left (Ehud Barak and the Labor Party, Yitzhak Mordechai and the new Center Party). But Netanyahu coped with the discrepancy and the challenge fairly easily.

For one thing, parts of the nationalist right wing and the settler movement made a conscious decision to support him personally despite his decision to sign the Wye Agreement, which had angered them. They were clearly still distrustful of both Netanyahu and Sharon, but as they saw it, a vote for Benny Begin was a wasted vote, and Netanyahu was likely to offer the Palestinians less than would Barak or Mordechai.

For another, Netanyahu is benefiting from a profound change in Israel's body politic, a change that was already apparent in earlier elections, most poignantly in 1996, and is now ever more significant. Three large groups—Israelis of Middle Eastern, particularly North African, extraction; Orthodox Jews; and many of the recent immigrants from the former Soviet Union—have tended to vote as a bloc for Likud's prime ministerial candidate. They came to perceive the Labor Party as representing the establishment, the "old elites," secularism, and a "soft" approach to security and to the Arabs, while Likud and its leader came to be seen as representing Israel's underprivileged people, a respect for religion and tradition, an emphasis on security, and a tough, virile attitude toward the Arabs. These perceptions are so deeply entrenched that they have not thus far been shaken by Netanyahu's role in the Wye River Conference and its consequences. It remains to be seen how the third contender in the 1999 election, Yitzhak Mordechai—Netanyahu's disenchanted defense minister, and a politician with evident appeal to Oriental and traditional Jews—will affect this pattern.

Should Netanyahu be re-elected, he is likely to encounter the same contradiction between policy and politics that has marked his previous tenure in office. In other words, if elected by a right-wing constituency he will find yet again that a right-wing government and right-wing policies will prevent him from advancing the peace process and will pit him and Israel against both the United

States and the Arab world. He might then seek to include at least one of his chief rivals in a national-unity government. Conversely, should either Barak or Mordechai be elected, he may discover that a government of the center and left cannot enjoy enough support for the difficult decisions called for in final-status negotiations with the Palestinians and in new negotiations with Syria. Thus a national-unity government is a likely outcome of the 1999 election.

At the risk of stating the obvious, I should emphasize that the likelihood of a national-unity government does not eliminate the significance of victory by any of the contending candidates. A mandate given by the Israeli public to Netanyahu or to one of his rivals, to the policies pursued by the current prime minister or those advocated by his challengers, is likely to differ markedly, even within the context of a national-unity government, and will send distinctly different messages to Israel's neighbors.

Whatever Israeli government is formed, it will have to formulate new peace policies. Fundamental and urgent decisions will have to be made with regard both to the Palestinians and to Syria-Lebanon.

On the Palestinian track, the immediate horizon will be defined by Arafat's anticipated statement that a unilateral declaration of statehood will be made in the fall unless an agreement is reached on final status or at least serious progress is made toward it. In any event he will insist on the implementation of the Wye Agreement, first and foremost the transfer of 13 percent of the West Bank to the Palestinian Authority's direct control. If re-elected, Prime Minister Netanyahu would be hard put to reject that demand without a serious crisis with the Palestinians and an acrimonious confrontation with the United States.

A different Israeli prime minister might argue that the original Oslo process has run its course and, given the imminence of Arafat's declaration of statehood and the need to put a serious negotiation in place quickly, that it makes sense to fit implementation of the Wye Agreement into this larger context. The effectiveness of such an approach would be contingent on success in persuading both the Palestinian leaders and the United States that Israel is genuinely committed to working toward an early final-status agreement. At that point both Israelis and Palestinians will have to think through all of the principal issues at stake: Palestinian statehood; the scope, jurisdiction, and powers of a Palestinian state; the future and status of Israeli settlements and settlers in the West Bank and the Gaza Strip; water resources; and, very significantly, refugees and the Palestinian insistence on their own "right of return."

It would be easy to argue that—given the weight and complexity of this daunting agenda, the mixed record of Israeli-Palestinian relations since 1993, the Israelis' domestic political configuration, and the limitations (objective and self-imposed) on Arafat's range of options—the prospects of Israeli-Palestinian final-status negotiations are dim. But other, countervailing considerations should brighten this pessimism. As I have noted, the informal Palestinian-Israeli negotiation conducted in 1995 by Abu Mazen and the Labor politician Yossi Beilin (then deputy foreign minister) concluded successfully with a draft agreement about final status. Yossi Beilin is to the left of

center in his own party, and what was acceptable to him
may not be acceptable to an Israeli majority, but he is an
important, mainstream politician. Abu Mazen is a very senior member of the Palestinian leadership's inner circle.
Even if their draft agreement is unacceptable as such, its
very existence is an encouraging sign.

Also, while wide gaps separate the Israeli and Palestinian positions on most key issues, each side has in fact accepted significant components of the other's position.
Several senior right-wing leaders in Israel have publicly
endorsed the idea of Palestinian statehood. It has been a
grudging endorsement, and the scope and powers imag-
ined for such a Palestinian state fall far short of Palestinian
expectations and red lines. But the principle has been established. This has been matched by the Palestinian leaders' resignation to the fact that most of the Jewish settlers
and settlements on the West Bank remain in place, under
Israeli control if not sovereignty, which means that part of
the West Bank will remain under Israeli control. (Arafat
probably thinks of some 10 percent of the territory. Israeli
aspirations, certainly on the right but also on the left, are
dramatically more ambitious.) Here, too, an important
principle has been established.

Finally, it is significant to note that the new Israeli-
Palestinian relationship has weathered three years of conflict, tension, and crisis. The two Oslo agreements created
a new reality, and both parties to the conflict have, however grudgingly, come to accept them. A web of vested
interests, relations, and expectations is there on which future negotiations can draw.

The Palestinian Authority governs about 2.5 million

Palestinians living in the West Bank and in the Gaza Strip. According to current estimates, these constitute about 40 percent of the Palestinian people. Two other large groups of Palestinians are citizens of Israel (where they constitute nearly 17 percent of the general population) and of Jordan (where they are a majority of the population); and almost a million Palestinians live as refugees in Lebanon, Syria, and Iraq. Their position is most precarious in Lebanon, where the Christian communities are likely to remain vehemently opposed to giving citizenship or legitimacy to some 400,000 people added to the Muslim majority. Smaller groups of Palestinians live in other countries in the Middle East and outside the region.

For many years Arafat and the PLO were regarded as primarily representing the Palestinian diaspora, the "outside." It has been one of the more intriguing consequences of the Oslo Accords that Arafat and his establishment became essentially a government of the West Bank and the Gaza Strip. This has not been Arafat's original vision, and it is probably not the role he assigns to himself. Insistence on Israeli acceptance, even in principle, of the Palestinian right of return would be an obvious measure for Arafat to choose for addressing this issue. It would give him at least some defense against the criticism that he has abandoned the refugees and the diaspora, as well as a mechanism for denying Israel the finality it craves.

Israelis react negatively to the Palestinians' espousal of their right of return precisely for this second consideration and for several other reasons. They rule out any Palestinian return, even a symbolic one, to Israel proper, and they

view any sizable influx of Palestinians to the West Bank
and Gaza as impractical. Nor do they accept the Palestinian argument that Israeli recognition of the right of return
is essential because it indicates acceptance of the Palestinians' just grievance. Most Israelis do not think their
country was born as the result of an "original sin," and
they feel that their cause and title are at least equal to the
Palestinian ones. In any discussion of the fundamental issues of the Israeli-Palestinian conflict, Israel will press this
perspective and point of view. And at some point, the
Palestinians' quest for early establishment of Palestinian
statehood will come into conflict with objections to their
insistence on a right of return. And Israel is not the only
state in the region sensitive to Arafat's, the PLO's, or the
PA's claim to represent the Palestinian diaspora. That
claim presents a challenge to Jordan, where sensitivity to
the issue has been all the more acute following King Hussein's death.

Israel's new government will also have to decide on its
Syrian policy. The natural tendency of any prime minister
would be to try to establish a sequence in the political and
diplomatic work for the peace process and to postpone negotiation with Syria until the conclusion (or, possibly, collapse) of a final-status negotiation with the Palestinians.
But this would be difficult not only because Assad will
surely resent any attempt to relegate his country to a secondary position, let alone to place him behind Arafat. Israel's predicament in Lebanon has reached such a degree
of difficulty, and has come to occupy such a prominent
place on the national agenda, that a new government will
have to deal with it—and perforce with Syria—early on.
In fact, in the election campaign the principal contenders

all committed themselves to early resolution of the
Lebanese issue.

Let us return to the problem of sequence in the peace
process. It is difficult to envisage any Israeli government,
however wide its base of support, making dramatic territorial concessions simultaneously in the West Bank and in
the Golan Heights. And yet any strategy or tactic seeking
to conclude one impressive deal and expecting to postpone or freeze the others is misguided. Not only would Israel's Arab partner-protagonists refuse to go along, but the
Israeli public would find it hard to pay the price of, say, a
final-status agreement with the Palestinians while continuing to sustain casualties in the north. So the strategy must
encompass both the framework of a comprehensive settlement and a tactical breakdown into components and
phases. The Israeli leadership will have to mobilize domestic support while at the same time dealing with Arab
partners determined to perpetuate ambiguity and open-
endedness, to fan the embers of a lingering conflict.

In meeting this challenge Israel's leaders will need two
principal partners. The United States will have to return
to playing its erstwhile role as orchestrator of the Arab-
Israeli peace process, fitting it into a larger scheme for the
Middle East. This means that new policies must be formulated with regard to Iran and Iraq. A policy on the
Middle East must be developed in which Turkey's new position is well fitted. A revived Arab-Israeli peace process
would create an opportunity to make a new regional order,
while, at the same time, a new regional order becomes the

larger context without which Arab-Israeli peace cannot flourish.

And, obviously, the partnership of most Arab states— the negotiating partners, the countries that have made peace with Israel, and other important actors like Saudi Arabia—is a sine qua non. But the Arab world is in a state of transition, and the awkward succession to the throne in Jordan is a harbinger of changes that will inevitably occur sooner or later in other long-established Arab regimes. At a more profound level, many social and economic developments, recent access to comparatively free and international media, the information revolution, and other technological changes are bound to create political changes. Amid all this, the Arab states will have to draw their own conclusions from the earlier phases of the peace process and deal differently with Israel, once Israel is ready for the task.

Beyond politics there lurk the underlying problems of the Middle East, first and foremost among them being the growing pressure of an exploding population on scarce resources. Israel's first efforts to offer the Arab world cooperation in meeting this challenge were misconstrued and became counterproductive. It is imperative now for Israelis and Arabs to find the formula for establishing the larger cooperative effort in which a durable political peace can be embedded.

Neither the Middle East as a region nor the Arab-Israeli conflict as a cluster of specific issues and problems lends itself to grand schemes or easy solutions. A swift transformation of the kind that took place in Eastern Europe when the Berlin Wall was toppled cannot be envisaged. This should be borne in mind while planning for a resolution of the Arab-Israeli conflict. Policy-makers should be guided by a concept of a comprehensive settlement, but they should be ready to implement it in phases, and despite crises and reversals. It is easy to be intimidated by the host of domestic and regional problems that are certain to clutter the path. Seeing through these obstacles to the peace ahead is, indeed, a task not for policy-planners and analysts but for leaders and statesmen.

NOTES

I. THE BACKGROUND

1. For two overviews of the Arab-Israeli conflict, see Elie Kedourie, "The Arab-Israeli Conflict," in *Arabic Political Memoirs* (London, 1974), pp. 218–31; Shimon Shamir, "The Arab-Israeli Conflict," in A. L. Udovitch, ed., *The Middle East: Oil, Conflict and Hope* (Lexington, Mass., 1976), pp. 195–231. For more detailed accounts, see Nadav Safran, *Israel—The Embattled Ally* (Cambridge, Mass., 1981); Don Peretz, *Palestinian Refugees and the Middle East* (Washington, D.C., 1993); Fred Khourie, *The Arab-Israeli Dilemma* (New York, 1968).

2. On the Madrid process, see James A. Baker, *The Politics of Diplomacy* (New York, 1995), pp. 417–20, 425–28, 447–49, 454–57, 459–63, 468–69, 487–89, 500–7; Eithan Ben Tzur, *Haderekh Lashalom Overet be Madrid* [The Road to Peace Goes through Madrid] (Tel Aviv, 1997).

3. For an original, classic account of the Cold War in the Middle East, see John Campbell, *Defense of the Middle East* (New York, 1960). For a subsequent complete study of U.S. policy in the Middle East and relations with Israel, see Steven Spiegel, *The Other Arab-Israeli Conflict* (Chicago, 1985).

4. See William Quandt, *A Decade of Decisions* (Berkeley, Calif., 1997).

5. See Benny Morris, *1948 and After* (Oxford, 1994); Avi Shlaim, *The Politics of Partition: King Abdallah, The Zionists and Palestine 1951–1971* (Oxford, 1990); Ilan Pappe, *The Making of the Arab-Israeli Conflict 1947–1951* (New York, 1988); Efraim Karsh, *Fabricating History: The New Historians* (London, 1997); Shabtai Teveth, "Charging Israel with Original Sin," *Commentary* 88 (September 3, 1989): 24–33; Zeev Sternhell, *The Founding Myths of Israel: Nationalism, Socialism and the Making of the Jewish State* (Princeton, 1998); Rami Tal, "No Subject Is Taboo for the Historian" (an interview with Anita Shapira), in Carol Diament, ed., *Zionism—The Sequel* (New York, 1998).

6. See Itamar Rabinovich, *The Road Not Taken* (New York, 1991); Neil Caplan, *Futile Diplomacy*, vol. 3 (London, 1997); Neil Caplan and Laura Zittrain Eisenberg, *Negotiating Arab-Israeli Peace* (Indiana, 1998).

7. For a cogent presentation of an Arab point of view, see Boutros Boutros-Ghali, "The Arab Response to the Challenge of Israel," in Udovitch, *The Middle East: Oil, Conflict and Hope*, pp. 231–50.

8. See Yehoshafat Harkabi, *Arab Attitudes to Israel* (Jerusalem, 1976); Yehoshafat Harkabi, *Arab Strategies and Israel's Response* (New York, 1977).

9. See Shimon Shamir, "The Middle East Crisis: On the Brink of War (14 May–4 June)," in D. Dishon, ed., *Middle East Record 1967* (Tel Aviv, 1971), pp. 183–204.

10. For a penetrating assessment of the major currents of opinions and the national mood in Israel, see Amos Oz, *In the Land of Israel* (London and New York, 1983).

11. See Fouad Ajami, *The Arab Predicament* (Cambridge, 1982).

12. See Helena Cobban, *The Palestine Liberation Organization* (Cambridge, 1984); Avraham Sela and Moshe Maoz, eds., *The PLO and Israel* (New York, 1997).

13. See Shlomo Avineri, *Israel and the Palestinians* (New York, 1971).

14. For the Israeli and American perspectives on the September 1970 crisis in Jordan, see Yitzhak Rabin, *The Rabin Memoirs* (Boston, 1979), pp. 186–89; Henry Kissinger, *The White House Years* (Boston, 1979), pp. 597–617. For a contemporary exposition of Likud's view that "Jordan is Palestine," see Benjamin Netanyahu, *A Place Among the Nations* (New York, 1993), pp. 343–45.

15. For a critical view of Israeli policy at the time, see Ezer Weizman, *On Eagles' Wings* (London, 1976), pp. 279–95.

16. See Zeev Laqueur, *Confrontation* (London, 1974).
17. See William B. Quandt, *The Peace Process* (Washington, D.C., and Berkeley, Calif., 1993); Malcolm Kerr, ed., *Rich and Poor States in the Middle East* (Boulder, Colo., 1982); Moshe Dayan, *Breakthrough* (New York, 1981).
18. See Kissinger, *Years of Upheaval* (New York, 1982), pp. 747–98.
19. See Rabin, *Memoirs*, pp. 253–300; Itamar Rabinovich, "The Challenge of Diversity: American Policy and the System of Inter-Arab Relations 1973–1977," in I. Rabinovich and H. Shaked, eds., *The Middle East and the United States* (New Jersey, 1980), pp. 181–96.
20. See Kissinger, *Years of Upheaval*; Rabin, *Memoirs*, pp. 799–853.
21. See Jimmy Carter, *Keeping Faith* (Toronto, 1982), pp. 269–429, and *The Blood of Abraham* (Boston, 1985); Cyrus Vance, *Hard Choices* (New York, 1983), pp. 16–256.
22. See Quandt, *Peace Process*.
23. See Zeev Schiff and Ehud Ya'ari, *Israel's Lebanon War* (New York, 1984); Itamar Rabinovich, *The War for Lebanon, 1970–1983* (Ithaca, N.Y., and London, 1984).
24. See Fouad Ajami, *The Dream Palace of the Arabs* (New York, 1998).
25. See Shimon Peres, *Battling for Peace* (London, 1995), pp. 258–70.
26. See Baker, *Politics of Diplomacy*; Uri Savir, *The Process* (New York, 1998); and Itamar Rabinovich, *The Brink of Peace* (Princeton, 1998).

II. MADRID AND OSLO: YEARS OF HOPE

1. Studies and memoirs regarding this period include Itamar Rabinovich, *The Brink of Peace* (Princeton, 1998); Uri Savir, *The Process* (New York, 1998); David Makovsky, *Making Peace with the PLO* (Boulder, 1996); Warren Christopher, *In the Stream of History* (California, 1998); Hanan Ashrawi, *This Side of Peace* (New York, 1995); Abbas Mahmud, *Through Secret Channels* (Reading, U.K., 1995).
2. See Joseph Alpher, "What Went Wrong?" (The American Jewish Committee, New York, 1998).
3. See Robert Slater, *Rabin of Israel* (London, 1996). See also the memoir by Rabin's widow, Leah Rabin, *Our Life—His Legacy* (New York, 1997).

4. For Baker's surprisingly brief version of this, see James A. Baker, *The Politics of Diplomacy* (New York, 1995), pp. 555–57.

5. See FBIS, July 27, 1992, pp. 5–6, "Final Statement Issued."

6. On Hamas and Islamic Jihad, see Ziad Abu-Amr, *Islamic Fundamentalism in the West Bank and Gaza* (Indiana, 1994); Hisham H. Ahmad, *From Religious Salvation to Political Transformation: The Rise of Hamas in Palestinian Society* (Jerusalem, 1994).

7. See Martyn Indyk, "Dual Containment," lecture at the Washington Institute, May 18, 1993.

8. See Yossi Beilin, *Laga'at BaShalom* [To Touch Peace] (Tel Aviv, 1997).

9. See Shimon Peres, *Battling for Peace* (London, 1995).

10. For a detailed version of this episode, see Rabinovich, *Brink of Peace*, pp. 108–15. My version of the event is contested by the Syrian view that Rabin actually "committed Israel to a withdrawal from the Golan." For the Syrian version, see Ambassador Walid Muallem's interview in *Journal of Palestine Studies* 26, no. 2 (Winter 1997): 401–12.

11. The only detailed account of the Israeli-Jordanian negotiations is in Moshe Zak, *Hossein Oseh Shalom* [Hussein Makes Peace] (Ramat Gan, 1996).

12. See Uri Savir, *The Process* [in Hebrew] (Tel Aviv, 1998), pp. 346–50.

13. See Shimon Peres, *The New Middle East* (New York, 1993).

14. See FBIS, October 12, 1995, pp. 50–61, "Radio on Al-Assad's *Al-Ahram* Interview."

15. See Shai Feldman, *Nuclear Weapons and Arms Control in the Middle East* (Cambridge, Mass., 1997), pp. 7–15, 153–58.

III. YEARS OF STAGNATION

1. See the official text: "The Wye River Memorandum Signed at the White House, Washington, D.C.," United States Information Center.

2. So far, two biographies of Benjamin Netanyahu have been published in Hebrew. I give their titles in English here: Ben Kaspit, *Netanyahu: The Road to Power* (Tel Aviv, 1997); and Ronit Vardi, *Bibi—Who Are You, Mr. Prime Minister?* (Jerusalem, 1997).

3. See the interview with him in *Ha'aretz*, September 18, 1998.

4. See Benjamin Netanyahu, *A Place Among the Nations: Israel and the World* (New York, 1993), pp. 256–328.

5. See ibid., pp. 350 ff.

6. See ibid., pp. 351–53.

7. For an illuminating study of the 1996 elections and their social context, see Daniel Ben Simon, *Another Country* [in Hebrew] (Tel Aviv, 1997); also Daniel J. Elazar and Shmuel Sandler, *Israel at the Polls: 1996* (London, 1998).

8. See Netanyahu's interviews with David Makovsky, *Jerusalem Post*, May 10, 1996, and with Shimon Schiffer, *Yediot Ahronot*, May 23, 1996.

9. See ibid.

10. See FBIS, May 23, 1996, "Likud Issues Platform," p. 4.

11. See interview with Makovsky, *Jerusalem Post*.

12. See FBIS, June 18, 1996, "Netanyahu Government Presents Basic Guidelines," pp. 32–36.

13. See FBIS, June 24, 1996, "Final Communiqué Issued by Arab Summit," pp. 13–16.

14. See Itamar Rabinovich, *The Brink of Peace* (Princeton, 1998), pp. 256–64.

15. See the chapters on Israel in Bruce Maddy Weizman, ed., *Middle East Contemporary Survey, 1996* and *1997* (Boulder, Colo., forthcoming).

16. For an excellent synoptic survey of the events that led to the signing of the Wye Agreement, see David Makovsky's article in *Ha'aretz*, December 4, 1998.

17. For a critical biography of Ariel Sharon, see Uzi Benziman, *He Does Not Stop at the Red Light* [in Hebrew] (Tel Aviv, 1985).

18. The document was first published in *Ha'aretz*, November 16, 1998.

IV. THE WEB OF RELATIONSHIPS

1. See Elie Kedourie, "The Arab-Israeli Conflict," in *Arabic Political Memoirs* (London, 1974), pp. 218–31; Shimon Shamir, "The Arab-Israeli Conflict," in A. L. Udovitch, ed., *The Middle East: Oil, Conflict and Hope* (Lexington, Mass., 1976), pp. 195–231.

2. See Shimon Shamir, ed., *Egypt from Monarchy to Republic* (Oxford, 1995); Israel Gershoni, *The Emergence of Pan-Arabism in Egypt* (Tel Aviv, 1981); and *Rethinking the Egyptian Nation: 1930–1945* (Cambridge, 1995).

3. See Abraham Sela, "The Question of Palestine in the Inter-Arab System, from the Foundation of the Arab League Until the Invasion of Palestine by the Arab Armies, 1945–1948" [in Hebrew], Jerusalem, 1986.

4. See P. J. Vatikiotis, *Nasser and His Generation* (London, 1978), *Conflict in the Middle East* (London, 1971), and *The History of Modern Egypt* (London, 1991).

5. See William B. Quandt, *The Peace Process* (Washington, D.C., and Berkeley, Calif., 1993).

6. See Fouad Ajami, *The Dream Palace of the Arabs* (New York, 1998).

7. On the nuclear dimension of Israeli-Egyptian relations, see Shai Feldman, *Nuclear Weapons and Arms Control in the Middle East* (Cambridge, 1997), pp. 206–24.

8. Of the many accounts of messages exchanged between Israel and Syria since May 1996, see the press statement issued on January 19, 1997, by Netanyahu's office clarifying such reports, and on July 22, 1998, about a meeting between Minister Ariel Sharon and settlers in the Golan Heights, during which Sharon told them about secret contacts between Israel and Syria to prepare for negotiation predicated on Israel's withdrawal in the Golan. See also the report produced by the Baker Institute for Public Policy at Rice University, "The Prospects for the Israeli-Syrian Peace Negotiations," June 1998.

9. Of the many reports on this visit, see the article by S'aid Badran in *Ma'ariv*, August 17, 1997.

10. For the history of Israel and the Zionist movement's contacts with various groups in Lebanon, see Laura Zittrain Aisenberg, *My Enemy's Enemy* (Detroit, 1994); Benny Morris, "Israel and the Lebanese Phalange: The Birth of a Relationship 1948–1951," *Studies in Zionism* 5, no. 1 (1984): 125–44.

11. See Ehud Ya'ari and Ze'ev Schiff, *Israel's Lebanon War* (New York, 1994); Itamar Rabinovich, *The War for Lebanon, 1970–1983* (Ithaca, N.Y., and London, 1984).

12. See Avi Shlaim, *Collusion Across the Jordan* (Oxford, 1988); Dan Shiftan, *Optzia Yardenit* [Jordanian Option] (Efal, 1986); Moshe

Zak, *Hossein Oseh Shalom* [Hussein Makes Peace] (Ramat Gan, 1996), and "Israel and Jordan: Strategically Bound," *Israel Affairs* 3, no. 1 (Autumn 1996): 39–60. See also Uriel Dann, *Studies in the History of Transjordan, 1920–1949* (Boulder, Colo., 1984).

13. See my *The Road Not Taken* (New York, 1991), pp. 111–67.
14. For a Jordanian version of the 1967 crisis and war, see Samir Mutawi, *Jordan in the 1967 War* (Cambridge, 1987).
15. See Asher Susser, *On Both Banks of the Jordan* (London, 1994).
16. See chapter 1, note 14.
17. The Constitution of the Hashemite Kingdom of Jordan, chap. 1, art. 1, as found in Muhammad Khalil, ed., *The Arab States and the Arab League* (Beirut, 1962).
18. See Harold H. Saunders, *The Other Walls* (Princeton, N.J., 1991).
19. For several classic statements of Israel's outlook on the Palestinians, see Shlomo Avineri, *Israel and the Palestinians* (New York, 1971).
20. For a sympathetic history of the Palestinian National Movement, see Helena Cobban, *The Palestine Liberation Organization* (Cambridge, 1984).
21. For two basic, and very different views on the subject, see Jacob Landau, *The Arabs in Israel: A Political Study* (London, 1969), and Ian Lustick, *Arabs in the Jewish State: Israel's Control of a National Minority* (Austin, Texas, 1980).
22. See Majid Al Haj and Henry Resenfeld, *Arab Local Government in Israel* (Tel Aviv, 1988); Jacob Landau, *The Arab Minority in Israel, 1967–1991: Political Aspects* (London, 1994); C. Klein, *Israel as a Nation State and the Problem of the Arab Minority in Search of a Status* (Tel Aviv, 1987); David Kretzmer, *The Legal Status of the Arabs in Israel* (Tel Aviv, 1987); Sammy Smooha, *Arabs and Jews in Israel*, 2 vols. (Boulder, Colo., 1989–92); Elie Rekhess, "Resurgent Islam in Israel," *Asian and African Studies* 27, nos. 1–2 (March–July 1993), and Rekhess, ed., "Arab Politics in Israel at a Crossroad," *Occasional Papers 119* (Tel Aviv, 1991); Nadim Ruhana, "The Political Transformation of the Palestinians in Israel from Acquiescence to Challenge," *Journal of Palestine Studies* 18 (1989).
23. A particularly radical version of this position was offered by Dr. Azmi Bishara, currently a member of the Knesset, in a lengthy interview he gave to *Ha'aretz*, May 29, 1998.
24. After the 1948 war, the Iraqi government conducted a study of the

Arab debacle in Palestine which offers important early insights into the Arab, and specifically Iraqi, view of the conflict. See Shmuel Segev, *In the Eyes of an Enemy* [in Hebrew] (Tel Aviv, 1954).

25. See Shmuel Segev, *The Iranian Triangle* (New York, 1988).

26. On the Iran-Iraq war, see Anthony H. Cordesman and Abraham R. Wagner, *The Iran-Iraq War* (Boulder, Colo., 1990). On Saddam's Iraq, see Efraim Karsh, *Saddam Hussein: A Political Biography* (London, 1991); Ofra Bengio, *Saddam Speaks on the Gulf Crisis* (Tel Aviv, 1992); Amatzia Baram, *Culture, History and Ideology in the Formation of Ba'thist Iraq, 1968–1989* (Hampshire, England, 1991); and Samir Al Khalil, *Republic of Fear: The Politics of Modern Iraq* (New York, 1990).

27. See Avner Yaniv, "Israel Faces Iraq: The Politics of Confrontation," in Amatzia Baram and Barry Rubin, eds., *Iraq's Road to War* (New York, 1996).

28. See *Al Thawra*, April 3, 1990. See also "President Warns Israel, Criticizes U.S., April 1, 1990," in Bengio, *Saddam Speaks on the Gulf Crisis*.

29. See Judith Miller and Laurie Mylroie, *Saddam Hussein and the Crisis in the Gulf* (New York, 1990).

V. PEACE AND NORMALIZATION

1. See Muhammad Sayyid [Sid] Ahmed, *After the Guns Fall Silent* (London, 1976).

2. See ibid., p. 67.

3. See ibid., p. 111.

4. See ibid., pp. 111–13 passim.

5. See ibid., p. 114.

6. See ibid., p. 115.

7. See Itamar Rabinovich, *The Road Not Taken* (New York, 1991), pp. 135–67.

8. The debate still continues as to whether an agreement could have been made and an opportunity was missed by Golda Meir's government in 1971. For a detailed account by a member of Meir's Cabinet, see Gad Ya'akobi, *On the Razor's Edge* [in Hebrew] (Tel Aviv, 1989).

9. See S. A. Sela, *The Decline of the Arab-Israeli Conflict* (Albany, N. Y., 1998), pp. 156–57.

10. Some of those ideas were put forth in the debate that followed the publication of Sid Ahmed's book. See *Al-Hawadith*, Beirut, May 30, June 13, June 20, 1975.

11. See Boutros Boutros-Ghali, "The Arab Response to the Challenge of Israel," in A. L. Udovitch, ed., *The Middle East: Oil, Conflict and Hope* (Lexington, Mass., 1976).

12. For impressions and reflections of an Israeli intellectual after a first visit to Egypt, see Amos Elon, *Flight into Egypt* (New York, 1980).

13. See *Ha'aretz*, January 7, 1999.

14. See Shimon Peres, *The New Middle East* (New York, 1993), p. 86.

15. See ibid., pp. 62–64.

16. See Patrick Seale, "Asad's Regional Strategy and the Challenge from Netanyahu," *Journal of Palestine Studies* 26, no. 1 (Fall 1997): 36.

17. See Fouad Ajami, *The Dream Palace of the Arabs* (New York, 1998).

18. Cited in ibid., pp. 256–58.

19. Edward Said, *The Politics of Dispossession* (New York, 1995), pp. 34, 45.

20. See Daniel Pipes, "Just Kidding," *The New Republic*, January 8 and 15, 1996, pp. 18–19.

21. See "Interview with President Assad," *Al-Ahram*, October 11, 1995, p. 1.

22. Thus the argument has been raised that "this reality was translated among Egyptian national security circles into a growing fear of the future. According to these circles the Egyptian market will be dominated by foreign powers, moreover by Israel. It has even been claimed that Israel will achieve economically what it has failed to achieve militarily." (Abdel Monem Said Aly et al., *National Threat Perceptions in the Middle East* [Geneva, Switzerland, 1995].)

23. See interview with Syrian television, November 16, 1997, quoted in *Al-Ra'y al-'Amm* (Kuwait), November 17, 1997.

24. See Radio Cairo, June 23, 1996.